Jac̶̶̶̶̶̶̶̶̶̶̶ cc

Twelve
Simple Words

the columba press

First published in 1994 by
ᴄhe ᴄoℓumʙʌ ᴘʀᴇss
93 The Rise, Mount Merrion, Blackrock, Co Dublin

Cover by Bill Bolger
Origination by The Columba Press
Printed in Ireland by
Genprint Ltd. Dublin.

ISBN 1 85607 119 7

Contents

Introduction

I remember, many years ago, beginning a course on the Pentateuch. I hadn't an idea what the course was about; all I knew was that it was a course that was necessary to meet graduation requirements. Anyhow, the first lecture lasted forty–five minutes, and, by then, the blackboard was covered with more Greek and Hebrew words than English. When I returned home that afternoon, I went straight to my room, found a pocket dictionary, and looked up the word 'Pentateuch', because the lecturer had been so busy talking about its derivation, and its history, that he never got around to telling us what the word meant! (It is a title for the first five books of the Bible, in case some of my readers still don't know!)

I am a teacher by training and by aptitude, and I take nothing for granted. I have chosen a dozen words, frequently used in religious contexts, and I have shared some insights and reflections on them. I think they are key words, the proper understanding of which could be very important on my journey through life. There is no particular order to the words, beyond my own instinctive selection, as I wrote. These words were chosen, obviously, to the exclusion of many other equally-important words. I had, of necessity, to be arbitrary in my choice, as I wrote within the scope of my time and talent.

I have culled a thought for reflection at the end of each chapter, in the hope that it might pull together, for the reader, the central theme being discussed and might serve as a catalyst for further thought, understanding and revelation. Maybe, once again, it is the teacher in me that continues to take nothing for granted, and believes in repetition as a tried and trusted way of learning! I am always conscious of a great desire to put in simple language the basic teachings of the gospels. Jesus said that his message would always be something that the intellectual and worldly-wise would have difficulty in grasping. He said it was for those with the heart of a child. Children love asking questions, and they always want to know what things mean, and how things work. Maybe I couldn't tell you much about the evolution and development of the Pentateuch, but I am happy enough, for now, to be able to tell you what the word means!

CHAPTER 1

Sin

As I said in the introduction, there is no particular order to these chapters. I begin with sin for no other reason than that it opens up many other topics that would automatically follow. In a way, I am coming from where I'm at, and sin is one of the key words in coming to an understanding of the human condition.

Right from the beginning, I suggest that, when I think of sin, I begin by seeing myself as the victim of sin; I think of sin as something that happened to me. We normally call this original sin. Because of this, I am fundamentally damaged, with a hole, as it were, in the ozone layer of my soul. This damage is irreparable, except, of course, to the Creator who can always re-create. I believe that, when I look at sin in this way, I can then look at my own personal sin against this background, and thus come to a much healthier, and a more realistic understanding of the human condition. Without the advantage of this perspective, I believe I would have all the ingredients I need to burden myself with guilt, and self-recrimination.

As I write these words, I am using a word-processor. I am a newcomer to this wonder of the technological age, and I am still at that stage where I tread wearily, and hope that nothing goes wrong! I have a friend at the other end of a phone, should any part of the equipment begin acting up on me. If the whole system, or any part of it broke down, I am not very likely to try taking it apart and fixing it!

A human being is vastly more complex, and when the system breaks down, or is found to be broken in any way, I wouldn't attempt fixing it. As with the word-processor, I get back to the supplier with my problem; I will call in the Creator, who alone really knows how the human system works, and how it can be set right again.

Jesus tells a story about a man who sowed good wheat in a field. Later that night, an enemy came and sowed weeds among the wheat. After some time, when the wheat began to appear, some of his servants saw that the weeds were appearing also. They came to him to enquire where the weeds had come from. 'Was that not good wheat you sowed?' He said that it was indeed good wheat. 'And where did the weeds come from?', they asked. He told them that an enemy had done this. They then asked if they might begin to pull up the weeds, and he would not allow them. He said that they would destroy the wheat in the process. 'Leave that to me', he told them. He said that he would take care of the weeds in his way, and that he would still be able to collect the good wheat when the time came.

I think of original sin as the weeds among the wheat. It was good wheat, just as, when God created us, he saw that we were good. And then an enemy, or Satan, came and tried to destroy that creation. Just as with the weeds among the wheat, there was harm done, but nothing was lost or destroyed. If the gospels say anything, they surely speak about God's concern for the wheat, and his plan for taking care of the weeds. The whole story of Jesus is about redemption, or buying us back from the control of the enemy. It is about rescuing, about saving, and about harvesting the good into his barns.

I said earlier that we are damaged, that we are broken. In a later chapter we will speak of Jesus coming among us, precisely because of that brokenness. 'If it's not broken, don't fix it', is wise advice. If we could 'fix' ourselves, Jesus would have had no need to come. Jesus shows an extraordinary compassion for human brokenness. I honestly believe that a fundamental condition for having any hope of understanding or living the gospel, must be a realistic acceptance of the simple facts about our damaged human condition. Love of the poor has always been held as central to Christian thinking and action. Making an option for the poor is a concept that is much spoken of, and promoted in recent times. There is a poor person in each one of us. There is someone who is the victim of evil, of a sin which I did not commit. I believe that a fundamental option for that poor person within is essential, before I can fully open out to the good news of the gospels.

I am not, at all, belittling or excusing personal sin, the sins which we ourselves do commit. This is a hard and solid fact, and it would compound our wrong-doing if we were to deny it. What I am saying, however, is that I will never be open to having anything done about this if I fail to see it against the background of my sinful and damaged condition. When weeds are sown, we should not be surprised if weeds begin to show. While not excusing my own responsibility for my sins, I believe that I should begin by looking at them as symptoms of a problem. Trying to deal with the symptoms, without getting to the problem, is like cutting the heads off thistles. They will grow again, and can even become more deep-rooted with each new growth. Unless the thistles are removed by the roots, in a literally radical way, there will be no change. In fact, Jesus says that 'the last stage of that person will be worse than the first'. Once again, I am saying that it must involve the original creator being allowed to totally re-create. 'I make all things new', says the Lord.

To be objective often implies holding something out at arm's length, and having a good look at it. Usually, this is relatively easy, because it involves some object, person, or behaviour that is outside of myself. It is much more difficult, however, when it involves a condition that is fundamentally part of me. It can be difficult to see the wood for the trees. Human nature can be very complicated, and there are layers upon layers of emotions, feelings, instincts, and drives. It is far too complex for me to handle by myself. When I buy some new piece of equipment, it is usually accompanied by the maker's instructions. These instructions can include diagrams and explanations of parts, some set-up and operational guidelines, and advice on what to do when faults or breakdowns occur.

I remember, some years ago, watching two young people unpacking and setting up a computer. With their own natural instinct for things electronic, and with the occasional glance at the instructions, they worked away at putting all the parts in place. They seemed to have total confidence that, if they followed the instructions, this thing was going to work. I continued to watch, with fascination, as they began to experiment with the various facilities of the computer. They seemed to be clearly aware of both its potential and its limitations. They didn't expect it to speak, or to project a movie on the screen. They seemed to have a fairly clear idea of what wouldn't work, or what would cause damage. I couldn't help reflecting on how fortunate and blessed they would be in life, if they had such an overall and basic understanding of the workings and vagaries of our human condition!

What God created was, and always is good. 'God don't make no junk!' is how someone described it one time. That original good is still good, even if pollutants of destruction got into the mix. An enemy did this, in a vain attempt to destroy the goodness of God's creation. If human history can teach us anything, it must surely be how good continues to overcome and conquer evil. Adam and Eve in the garden seemed a disaster, but St Augustine would later proclaim, 'Oh happy fault that merited so great a Redeemer!' Calvary would seem like a victory for evil over good, yet God turned it into one of the most significant blessings in the history of humankind. My human condition can be a case of the glass being half-full or half-empty, of being faced with a problem or an opportunity.

In a later chapter, I will speak of God's acceptance of me as I am. When God created something he *saw* that it was good. When the good wheat was found to be polluted with weeds, God also saw that to be a fact. His concern, however, was for the wheat, and he was fully committed to harvesting that good wheat at the end of the day. He didn't pretend that things were other then they were; he just hoped that the workers wouldn't take on something that was totally beyond them. 'Leave that to me', was his request.

Basically, I am more sinned against than sinning, and only when I, too, am prepared to live within the world of that reality, can I begin to be open to God, and to his plan. I am a sinner. It is part of who and what I am. If I went to live at the North Pole. I would still be an Irishman! No piece of paper, or decree of government can alter that simple fact. I cannot run away from who or what I am. An acid test of my maturity is my ability to live with, and accept, the person that I am. Only God is good, as Jesus told the rich young man. Only God is perfect, and without flaw or imperfection. Original sin included the pride that would cause a mere creature to want to be equal to the Creator. To reject or to condemn myself for my human imperfection is to continue to repeat that original sin.

A man went to a doctor one time with a very real worry. He explained to the doctor that every part of himself that he touched was very sore, and he was worried. If he touched his nose, his knee, his elbow, all parts were very sensitive to touch, and were quite painful. The doctor gave him a full physical check-up, and when he was finished, the man asked the doctor if he had discovered what was wrong with him. 'Yes', said the doctor, 'I have. Your finger is broken.' Once the man knew what was wrong with him, and got that attended to, he was delighted that the other parts were no longer painful. It is absolutely necessary for me to realise 'what's wrong with me'. Otherwise, I will be pre-occupied with that, and, so, can only get worse.

I would strongly suggest that a healthy way of

being, and of living, is to fully accept the facts as they are, without any desire or attempt to cover-up or deny. It is to accept that, just as creation is the unique work of God, so is re-creation. Only God can do God's work! He can, of course, use anything or any person he chooses as instruments or channels through which he can do that work, but an electric wire is not a generator. God's Spirit is a spirit of truth, and can work most effectively in an atmosphere of truth. The more I am willing to be open to truth, and to things as they really are, the more effective God can be in my life. Looking at myself, and accepting what I see, and how things are, is a basic step towards encountering, and entering into a redeeming and re-creating relationship with our God of infinite love and unconditional acceptance.

St Paul has much to say to us about our human condition. This is all the more remarkable, because he began in life as a very religious person, totally tied up in rules, and perfection-seeking. Getting things perfect would be of obligation to him, and he would be very intolerant of human imperfections. He saw his salvation in the perfect observance of law, and in a perfectionistic approach to everything. The transformation that took place in him, after his conversion on the road to Damascus, was extraordinary. Gone was the self-righteousness of the Pharisee, to be replaced with a profound consciousness of his imperfections. In fact, he went so far as to claim that his human condition, with all of its brokenness, was his greatest claim to God's love and acceptance. He rejoiced in his weakness, because he believed that God's power is seen at best in weakness. Not for him was the self-scourging of the religious perfectionist, who takes all responsibility for human brokenness as a personal burden. He knew that God is always in control, and that, in him, there is never rejection of any part, or any person in his creation. He made a 180° turn from the blindness of the self-righteous, to the total acceptance of what he found in himself. I must stress, however, that it was only after receiving an out-pouring of the Spirit of truth, that such a turn-about was possible.

In summary, then, I can say that, because of my damaged nature, I am incapable of lifting myself out of the quick-sands of my own selfishness, and sinful condition. Only God can do that. I am not capable of raising myself towards God in any way; therefore, God, in his love, decided to come to where I am, to meet me there. We call this Incarnation, and I will deal with that in the following chapter.

Summary for Reflection

The first sin was committed against us, and we will never be able to relate properly to our human condition, unless we see as ourselves as, primarily, the victims of sin.

CHAPTER 2

Incarnation

I am an incarnate. In other words, I am living in a body. When my heart and other bodily organs cease to function, I will leave the body, and become a discarnate. To become incarnate is to begin to live in a body. The body has its origin in the clay of the earth, and the Latin for clay is *humus*. I, therefore, am a *human*. *Humilitas* is the Latin for 'of the earth', and *humility* is simply accepting the truth about my humanity, and its very definite limitations.

God is love. Everything that God does is prompted by love. God could have loved us from a distance, but he decided not to. Real love is going to where another person is, and accepting that person just as he is, and where he is. God decided to come to us. It is, once again, like Mohammed and the mountain. We couldn't go to God, so he decided to come to us. This was a profound and, literally, down-to-earth expression of his love and his accept-ance of us as we are. To come to some kind of revelation about the extraordinary event of

Incarnation is to enter into the very heart of the gospels. It is important, however, to remember, as Jesus said to Peter, 'Flesh and blood cannot reveal this to you, but my Father who is in heaven.'

There is a programme on television about sheep-dog trials. It is a programme that I enjoy. There are very few animals as stubborn as a sheep, and I am always fascinated to see the battle of wits between a flock of sheep and a good sheep-dog. Now imagine what would happen if the dog could speak in a language that the sheep could understand! The dog could explain that he is not out to harm them in any way, and that all he is trying to do is guide them to a particular place. If the sheep could understand why the dog is doing what he's doing, and what it is he hopes to achieve, then there might be a much smoother and effective encounter! This is a very lame attempt to illustrate the fact that God came among us to speak our language, and to explain to us just how he wants to enter into our human condition, and to guide our feet into the way of peace.

John the Baptist's father Zachary sang about the Lord coming to visit his people, and to redeem them. He was speaking about the greatest love-story ever told. Jesus spoke about lost sheep, and about a son who got it all wrong, and who came home to love and acceptance. He stressed that he had not come to condemn the world, but to save it. He spoke a language to which the most broken of human beings could easily relate.

What God created was good. The effect of original sin is that three main pollutants entered into his creation, that were not part of his design. Those evils were sin, sickness, and death. Jesus came to take on those three evils personally. He would clearly prove that he could forgive sin, cure sickness, and overcome death. Life can be very difficult at times. At best, it is a journey of many tensions; tensions between what I want to do, and what I ought to do, between what I want, and what I really need. All of these tensions and struggles are our own personal experience of the human condition. It is not easy for the human mind to grasp the width and the depth of what Jesus actually took on. The meeting of the human and the divine was dramatically signified in Jesus' baptism in the river Jordan. By lining up with sinners to be baptised, he was taking on the whole mess, as it were. He who was without sin became sin at that moment. No wonder John the Baptist was shocked, and protested.

However, when Jesus came up out of the water, the heavens were opened. That is a very significant phrase, because the heavens had been closed to us since the fall – that was part of original sin. And now, as the heavens opened, the Spirit of God came upon him, and Jesus was publicly confirmed by the Father as his go-between, as the meeting place for the Creator and his sinful creatures.

When I say that Jesus took on human nature, I mean that he took on *my* nature. I can go aside and reflect at great length about my personal experience of my own struggles, brokenness, and general human condition. If I then bring the reality of Incarnation into that formula, then I must accept that Jesus is actually in the midst of all that I am, and he is, at this very moment, effecting my salvation and redemption. 'The kingdom of God is within you,' Jesus said.

There is just one problem in all of this. God doesn't *give* me anything, he *offers* me everything. The magic key to all of his treasures is my 'Yes'. Without my permission, God can do nothing for me, or with me. 'I stand at the door and knock. If anyone opens the door, I will come in … and I will make my home there.' Jesus is, as it were, in the midst of all the sin and brokenness, and he is on constant stand-by, with JCBs and earth-movers, ready to move in at my request, at the first sign that such is my wish.

The average person walking down the road now believes in God, but not all are convinced that they need him just now. It is a special grace of God to come to a deep conviction of my own inability to 'fix' myself. God created me, and when things go wrong with me, only God can re-create, and make things right again. I am totally subject to the law of gravity, and I am not capable of raising myself out of the quick-sands of my own selfishness and self-will run riot. 'Peace on earth to those of good will' was the song of that first Christmas night. It is never a question of will-power. If I have the will, God will supply the power!

That is why I chose to write in the previous chapter about the human condition, before dealing with Incarnation. It is a fact of life that nothing short of God's direct intervention can effect any permanent improvement in how I am. Human effort may improve or change things for a while, but, because to be human is to be mortal, the results of that effort will also be mortal, and will not last. Only God is constant. 'Jesus is the same yesterday, today, and forever.'

God's thinking behind Incarnation must be that, from his view of things, it is patently obvious that, by ourselves, we just haven't a hope. God lays great emphasis on free-will, and our right to be involved in deciding our own destiny. He gives us nothing, while offering us everything. He won't send me to hell or heaven when I die; rather will he eternalise whatever decisions I make now. 'God helps those who help themselves' is a much-quoted phrase. What I am saying here, however, is that, then it comes to salvation, redemption, and any kind of permanent improvement of the human condition, then this is God's work, and his only. My contribution is to allow him act, by handing over to him, or by getting out of the way. The most important and basic thing I have to do is to stop playing God. God becomes God in my life the very moment I stop playing God. Then, and only then, can miracles begin to happen.

Grace builds on nature, it doesn't replace it. A spirituality of former times laid great emphasis on denying my human nature, and thus implying that, by my own efforts I could discipline and thus redeem it. This approach stressed rising above my humanity, by some superhuman effort on my part. It implied denying what was really there by stomping it under foot, and rising above it so much, to become so heavenly as to be no earthly good. Unfortunately, that came to be called holiness! I would contend that holiness is allowing God enter fully into my brokenness, to confront me with every dimension of it, and to open me to the possibility of naming, claiming, and taming every demon within me. If, after original sin, Adam and Eve had come before God and said 'Lord, we blew it!', I believe that God might well have smiled, and said 'That's OK, I'll take care of that.' What happened, however, was that Adam blamed Eve, and Eve blamed the devil! We're doing that since...

I quoted Zachary, John the Baptist's father, earlier, as he sang about God coming to visit his people. Incarnation was not just a once-off event. It is *now*, and it involves me. God came to Adam and Eve in the garden, and asked them what happened. All he wanted to hear was the truth, a simple answer to his question. Jesus walked around the Galilee countryside, and he asked many searching questions. 'Where is your husband?', he asked the woman at the well. 'What were you discussing as you walked along?' was the question he asked his disciples. He has the knack of looking right into the heart of a situation, and of asking a simple and searching question, that goes right to the heart of the matter. If the answer to his question is the truth, then his power can be totally effective. Not to face up to the truth is to shut the door against him, and reject his offer. Jesus cried as he looked across the Kedron valley at Jerusalem, and said, 'Salvation was within your grasp, and you would not accept it.' It is with a heavy heart that he sees any lack of openness on my part, something that limits his ability to work his redemption and salvation in me. When he came back to Nazareth, he could not work any miracles there, because of their lack of faith. His response was sadness rather than condemnation. He made it very clear, on more than one occasion, that he came to save, not to condemn.

Peter was shocked that Jesus knelt at his feet with a basin of water and a towel. When he recoiled in horror, telling Jesus that he would never allow him wash his feet, as if he were his slave, Jesus replied that, unless Peter allowed Jesus come to him, and love him in this way, he could not be one of his disciples. Jesus is totally down-to-earth, meeting people exactly as they are. Jesus wants to enter into the darkest corners of my being. He doesn't want to be treated like a visitor, when 'he visits his people, and redeems them.' We tend to bring a visitor into the front parlour, or sitting-room, which is in some sort of reasonable order. We certainly wouldn't let them into the kitchen, or the bedrooms, if they were in any kind of disarray. Jesus loves to be allowed feel at home, be at home, and make his home in the human heart, and he himself will take care of anything there that needs his forgiveness, healing, or redemption. He has come to set us free. We say, 'Lord, by your cross and resurrection, you have set us free. You are the saviour of the world.'

With some forms of spirituality, more than others, it is difficult for God to become incarnate! There is a religious pride that foolishly involves us at the heart of our own salvation. We tend to push God back into the sky, as it were, as we fill the void with saints, relics, and novenas! We have a stubbornness that insists on us doing our own 'saving', and we then expect God to approve our efforts and to pin a victory medal on us! When Jesus came that first Christmas night, there were many doors closed against him, and many people who just didn't want to know. Incarnation is nothing less than God himself offering to come among us, to take on all of our brokenness, to rescue and redeem us, and bring us safely back home to the Father. It is the greatest possible offer that God could make. After that, he stands back and awaits our reply. Everything depends on whether we have enough grasp of truth and reality to accept that offer, to do things his way, and allow him to be God. Original sin, trying to be as good as God, is a sin that continues to plague us, unless we allow Jesus to free us from such a kingdom of deceit, lies, and darkness, and lead us into his kingdom of truth, love, and life.

Summary for Reflection

God comes among us, in Jesus Christ, and offers to take all of the out-fall of original sin on himself, and to bring us safely back home to the Garden.

CHAPTER 3

Brokenness

We will now have a close-up look at the human condition, and, this time, we will include our personal sins, and all those things in us that are potentially destructive. Once again, we will look at this against the background of our sinful condition, resulting from original sin. To do otherwise would be a path to discouragement, guilt, and despair! Because of our damaged nature, there is some sort of basic rebelliousness within us that seems always to get in the way of our path to God. St Paul was very definite about how he experienced this. 'We know that the law is spiritual, but I am full of human weakness, sold as a slave to sin. I cannot explain what is happening to me, because I do not do what I want, but, on the contrary, the very things I hate … I know that nothing good lives in me, I mean, in my flesh. I can want to do what is right, but I cannot do it. In fact, I do not do the good I want, but the evil I hate … My inmost self agrees and rejoices with the law of God, but I notice in my body another law challenging the law of the Spirit, and delivering me as a slave to the law of sin, written in my members.' Paul has much more to say, along these lines, and if we stopped reading this passage too soon, we might think of him as being in the depths of despair. However, he concludes by rejoicing in the fact that Jesus, through Incarnation, and all that followed, has taken care of all that.

At this stage I need to say something that will be repeated many times throughout these pages: the only real sin for a Christian is not to have hope. It is basic to the Christian message that, no matter how hopeless a situation is, no matter how bad things really are, there is nothing that God cannot turn completely around, and set in the other direction.

One way of looking at our condition is to imagine some sort of leaden weight deep within us, that weighs us down and prevents us having any kind of lift-off. In more ways than one, we are subject to the law of gravity! The spirit, indeed, may be willing, but the flesh is very weak. There can be a constant break-down between the resolve and the carrying out of that resolve. 'The road to hell is paved with good intentions', is a phrase with which most of us can identify. All diets begin next Monday, and, please God, by then we'll have found some new excuse for delaying the pain until some other time! I heard about a man who read so much about the dangers of smoking that, one day, he made a firm resolution and gave up reading! Our behaviour would be funny, if it were not often pathetic. It is important to remember that it is not a question of will-power. It is a question of God supplying the power, as soon as I have the will! 'Peace on earth to those of good will' is a message that continues to ring throughout the story of salvation.

There is a story of a man who went to work each day with his lunch-box under his arm. Every day, in the canteen at lunch-time, he went through the same routine. He opened the box, took our a sandwich, separated the slices of bread, and moaned, 'Oh no, not cheese again today!' His pals were fed-up with this daily ritual, so one day a fellow worker said to him, 'Why don't you ask your wife to put something else in the sandwiches?' 'What wife?' the man replied, 'I'm not married.' 'Well then, who makes the sandwiches?' 'I do,' was the reply.

Part of our sinful condition is a kind of persistent blindness to the reality of things. It's like an alcoholic who, as often as not, is the last person in the world to see what others have seen for years. Part of the disease is that it tends to lead us to deny its existence.

There is a kind of insanity about our behaviour, and it can be difficult, if not impossible, for us to see it. This insanity shows itself through a persistent stubbornness that drives us to repeat the same mistakes, and to expect a different result each time! If I 'bridle' at the accusation of insanity, maybe I might concede that my behaviour, at times, is insane behaviour.

It may be easier to see our behaviour against the back-drop of love, the love we have in mind when we refer to God. That love is based on gentleness, truth, sincerity, and all that is best for us. Our own behaviour, at times, would prompt one to think that we were fully bent on our own self-destruction. In this is our insanity. Quite often, I reflect that I may well be more stupid than evil!

The story of the fall, or original sin, is best summed up thus: our first parents fell for a lie, and came under the management of darkness and deceit. They hid, and we are hiding since. The only antidote for us is truth, and the truth will set us free. This truth involves taking responsibility for our actions, and being willing to see things as they really are. Jesus told us that he never said anything unless the Father told him to tell us. When he told us a story, like the story about the prodigal son, he did so because the Father told him to tell us. The highlight of the story is when 'the son came to his senses', when he opened his eyes, and saw things as they really were. He was shocked at what he saw, and it was obvious to him that there was no future in going any further down that road. He did wrong, he was wrong, and he said so. Jesus assures us that there is a hug waiting at the end of that road of return, even if we did get pig's food all over our faces. It is an invitation back to the Garden, back to the security that accompanies truth.

The basic truth is that I just cannot 'manage' my life, from the time I was carried into a church to be baptised, until I am eventually carried into a church in a coffin! By myself, I am more part of the problem than I am of the solution. It is one of the greatest human paradoxes to say that my strength lies in recognising and accepting my weakness. If I am to travel anywhere in life, I must begin from where I am. In God's extraordinary economy, whatever I have is enough, if I am prepared to get down into my own reality, and not continue to live in 'cloud cuckoo land', with my head in the skies. Any compassion I have has come out of an experience of my own brokenness. It is from this that all empathy and mutual understanding flows. The Christian message speaks of acknowledging my own brokenness, and leaving my neighbour alone!

At Mass, I am allowed use the first person singular on only three occasions: 'I confess ... I have sinned ... Lord, I am not worthy ...'. All the rest is plural. When it comes to sin, I speak for myself, and about myself. That is why all judgements and condemnations are wrong. I am asked to take responsibility for my own behaviour, and to answer for that. It requires great maturity to be able to say 'I was wrong.' How much bloodshed and tears this world would be spared if someone somewhere was prepared to admit that he or she was wrong.

Guilt is not from God. 'I did not come to condemn the world ... Neither do I condemn you', are the words of Jesus. Being intolerant of my own brokenness and imperfections is a dangerous form of destructive pride. 'There is nobody good but God', Jesus told the rich young man. Getting in touch with my own brokenness, and not going beyond that would have all the ingredients for total despair. However, the idea behind the exercise is, that, the more aware I am of my own brokenness, the more open I will be to the redemption, salvation, healing, and forgiveness offered by Jesus. The more powerlessness I experience in my life, the more I may be open to the power of God. Sin and grace go hand in glove in the economy of God's salvation. 'Where sin abounds, there grace abounds still more' is a spiritual adage of long standing.

If we look at some of the miracles in the gospels we will see a few common characteristics in most of them. The first one is that the person concerned has exhausted all human resources at his or her disposal. The little woman in the crowd had spent eighteen years, and every penny she had, all to no avail. The man at the pool had spent thirty-eight years hoping against hope that something would happen. Jairus did all he could for his daughter, and she was still going to die. When the person concerned finally came to the conclusion that 'Whatever I'm doing, whatever I have, is not enough', then they were ready to bring things one step further. They turned to Jesus with a cry, 'If I can only touch the hem of his garment, I will be healed 'say but the word, and my servant will be healed ... At your word I will let down the net.' That was the second condition for a miracle, and, of course, the miracle followed.

Jesus tells a simple story in the gospels about two different approaches to God. It is the story of the Pharisee and the publican. The pharisee was totally convinced of, and pre-occupied with his own goodness, and righteousness. He wanted to tell God just how good he was, and God was expected to listen, and give his approval. He went further still in his arrogance when he began to compare his goodness to the sins of the publican at the back. The publican, on the other hand, was all too deeply conscious of his own sinfulness, especially in the presence of the all-holy God. He was a sinner, and he was deeply aware of that fact. He had none of the religious posturing of the Pharisee; he saw things as they really were, and he was not at all into the business of covering up or pretending. Jesus said that the publican was 'justified', in other words, he was someone in whom, and with whom God could relate. His cry, 'Oh God, be merciful to me, a sinner,' was a prayer that resounded around heaven. It is not possible for a human being to fall on his knees, cry out to God, and not be heard. The publican was a man of truth, and God's power is most effective in such people.

Most of my generation were 'programmed' with all the rules the Pharisees inherited, and we were told very definitely that if we kept all those rules we would be saved. I do not belong in the holy of holies! We aim for spiritual progress, not spiritual perfection. It's a long journey from where the Pharisee is, back to the publican, where I belong. If I were really convinced of my own brokenness and sinfulness, my attitude towards others would change dramatically. Gone would be the judgements, the condemnations, and the self-righteousness. I would open both hands fully, to ensure that neither is holding a stone to throw at anyone! If I fail to understand this basic truth, then I'm bound for all sorts of guilt-trips, when I find that life seems to be actually bringing me back towards the publican, rather than remaining with the Pharisee! What may look like failure is often spiritual growth. In other words, that's what is supposed to happen, provided that, when I'm back with the publican, I fall on my knees, and acknowledge the reality of that fact. I know it is total fantasy, but I sometimes reflect on how things might have been had I died in the full flush of my novitiate fervour many years ago! I know that the Lord would have been full of understanding, as I set out to convert the whole world (all the others!) to him. Now, however, I am truly grateful to have lived long enough to see where salvation was most needed! Maybe now, because of a realistic conviction of my own sinfulness, the Lord may be able to use me to help others turn back to him. If my own brokenness, and a positive acceptance of it, brings me to have enough compassion and genuine love for others then, please God, I may well be able to share some of the Lord's love and compassion with my fellow sinners along the way. I sometimes think that life is not about arriving anywhere, or becoming anything. Experiencing the brokenness and powerlessness along the way could well be an end in itself. In that sense, I believe that it is the depth of my life, rather than the length of it, that really matters.

Holiness is a word that can seem very abstract, and 'unearthly', whereas *wholesomeness,* or *wholeness* may be easier to understand. It is about being complete, about coming together, rather than being scattered, all over the place, and badly in need of getting myself together. 'Make friends with your shadow' is a much-acclaimed book of some years ago. The shadow is the part of self that I reject, the part that I hide from others, that I condemn, and that I frequently deny. It is only when I acknowledge the shadow, and strive to bring that out into the light, through acceptance, that I can become whole. It is about reconciliation. How the Lord's heart would thrill if the Pharisee was prepared to go down to the back, to embrace the publican; if the older brother was prepared to embrace the prodigal son; if Martha could have accepted Mary, and if Cain had not needed to kill his brother Abel. There is not a bullet fired, or a bomb planted, on this earth, that did not begin in the heart of an individual. If there is ever to be peace on this planet it must begin from within the hearts of people, and it cannot begin there until each of us becomes personally reconciled to all that is broken and in need of acceptance and reconciliation within the heart of each of us.

Summary for Reflection

A necessary ingredient for salvation is to be convinced beyond all doubt that I am someone who is badly in need of being saved!

CHAPTER 4

Religion

Religion, in its literal meaning, is about being bound to a set of rules and obligations. It has more to do with binding, than freeing. It has more to do with external practice than inner belief. In a sense, it is more or less a man-made phenomenon, rather than something that comes from God. Spirituality is about action in the heart, and is purely the work of God's spirit. Religion, I'm afraid, is very much of this earth, and, over the years, it has accumulated much of the pollutants that are part of everything earthly!

Religion is, essentially, about *law*. Moses wrote that if a person could be thoroughly good all his life, never yield to temptation, and never sin once, only then could he be saved. Pity the 'religious' people, who inherited such an ideal! Such an approach produced the Pharisees, whose whole thrust was to keep every minute detail of the Mosaic law. The Hebrews had a specific group, known as Scribes, whose whole purpose was to study and apply the law to every aspect of daily life. St Paul tells us that he had been one of the most religious persons of his day, striving with all his might to keep every single detail of Mosaic law. That was, of course, before Jesus came along to bring people across a bridge from a love of law to a law of love.

Religion has always tended to be destructive. It has had more to do with controlling than converting, with capturing, rather than captivating. Jesus came to free us from the burden of the law, but, unfortunately, many centuries later, evidence of a stubborn adherence to the letter of the law has survived in many religious denominations. Jesus said that he didn't come to *destroy* the law, but to *fulfil* it. Law is not bad in itself. In fact, law is there to protect and to promote what is best. Speed limits on vehicles driving through a town, or having to lead and muzzle a pit-bull terrier in a public place, is a good thing. It is not the law itself that is at issue, it is *why* it is there. It is when law and salvation become synonymous that we are losing sight of gospel teaching. The law helps in promoting right order, but it can never *save us*. To describe salvation as the outcome of keeping rules and regulations is to negate everything that the life, death, and resurrection of Jesus stands for. Adherence to law as a means of salvation is a stubborn expression of pride and arrogance, that runs counter to the whole concept of salvation as *gift*.

Religion can be both dangerous and destructive, because of a stubborn independence that is part of our condition, resulting from original sin. Part of what is 'wrong' with us is that we can insist on doing things our way, no matter what Jesus said. Jesus could never convert a Pharisee, because the Pharisees were too convinced of their own rightness and righteousness. The Pharisee in the temple was so busy telling God how good he was, that he had no time to listen to what God might have to say to him! It was more a question of 'Listen, Lord, your servant is speaking', than 'Speak, Lord, your servant is listening'! I think of Jesus, tongue in cheek, as it were, as he says that 'the Pharisee stood up and prayed thus *to himself* …'! In other words, what he had to say was more important to him than anything anyone, including God, might have to say. Religion, in fact, can lay greater stress on what we are doing for God than on anything God could do for us.

Religion is external, and it is what we do. In Ireland, we sometimes refer to 'practising our religion'. It is something we can learn, and become good at. It is about achieving and maintaining certain fixed standards, which can be very manipulative and controlling. It can expose us to great guilt trips for the inevitable failures that are part and parcel of our human journey. Only God is perfect, only God is holy, and only God is consistent, today, yesterday, and always. It is our own personal version of original sin when we try to be as good as God through some external practices of perfection. The fact is that we are always in conflict, we are always struggling with our human imperfections, we are always dealing with sin and brokenness; and anything that enables us rise above that is total *gift*, that we can neither possess nor earn. Salvation is based on the divine initiative, and it must never be turned into human endeavour. There can be no such thing as muscular Christianity, and, if I want to be a Christian, I must resign at once from the white-knuckle club!

A school teacher from Ireland died recently, and arrived at the gates of heaven. He was about to walk in when Peter stopped him. Peter explained that they were trying out a new system, where points, earned through human endeavour, would be included in assessing whether someone should be allowed into heaven or not. He explained to the teacher that a thousand points were required for entrance. He asked the teacher to list out what he had done that might merit heaven. The teacher stuck out his chest, and with total confidence, announced that he had been to Mass every day for fifty years. Peter took a note of that, and remarked, 'Very good ... that's one point.' The teacher's heart sank to his boots. 'O.K.', said Peter, 'what else did you do?' 'I worked with third-world agencies, St Vincent de Paul Society, and on many other charitable endeavours', replied the teacher. 'Very good', said Peter, 'that's another point.' The teacher was deeply shattered, and muttered to himself, 'It seems that it's only by the grace of God I'm going to get in there.' Peter heard him, and replied, 'If you really believe that, go on in, because that is the thousand points. Really believing that it is completely a gift from God is the biggest requirement for getting into heaven.'

'To live is to change, and to become perfect is to have changed often', wrote Cardinal Newman. Religion and religious people can have a really serious problem with change. Things must remain the way they have always been. Religious people are forever harping back to the way things were, 'before all these changes came.' Their security, and, many would believe, their salvation, lies in clinging to the way things were. They cannot deal with change, even though a good test of maturity is how one survives in the midst of change. 'We don't do that here' is the old trotted-out excuse for maintaining the *status quo*. It is more a question of maintenance than mission. Religion can block out much of God's on-going revelation, and can seriously impede one's personal growth.

A sin is a sin, and if God wanted a permissive society, he would have given us Ten Suggestions, instead of Ten Commandments. However, our understanding of it is always evolving. When I was a child, we had two reserved sins, from which the bishop alone could absolve, namely, making poteen (illegal spirits), and going to dances during Lent. It is no longer a sin to eat meat on Fridays, or to eat food after midnight, prior to receiving Communion. There would be less stress today on *what* I do, and more on *why* I did it. I could visit someone in hospital for several very different reasons. One could be that I feel genuinely sorry for the person, and I want to show that concern. Another might be that I have been waiting for years to see that person in hospital, and I'm determined not to miss this opportunity to see this for myself. Religion tends to be interested in the externals, in the facts, in the legal aspects of what happened, without reference to the spirit. Everything must *appear to be correct*; literal correctness is the virtue. Jesus slated the Pharisees for this approach. They laid great stress on the outside of a cup being clean, even if the inside was dirty and badly stained. They were, Jesus said, like whited sepulchres, that looked lovely on the outside, and inside were full of rotting material. Jesus condemned the Pharisees for parading their virtue for the approval of others. It is significant that Jesus ended up being killed by such religious people, because there was no way they were going to change. Jesus would have had more success in converting a prostitute than a Pharisee.

Religion has had a very bad press down through the years. It has often been seen as divisive and destructive, and it has produced such pseudo-Christian monstrosities as the Crusades and the Inquisition. It is frightening how a simple message of love and forgiveness can be manipulated to mean anything other than that, by self-righteous bigots and zealots. There is not a war in today's world that is not religious in some way – all killing each other in the name of religion. Religious bigotry, even when sweetly coated, is a very subtle and sinister form of violence. Evil is most evil, when it is disguised as good. The Church has never been good in its dealing with 'sinners'. Young girls who became pregnant outside marriage, were locked away in institutions for life, while their babies were removed from them without any consideration of the injustice involved. When someone committed suicide, a church funeral was denied. The list goes on and on. All of this was wrong, very wrong, and should be seen as such. It would be obscene to attempt to justify this, even, and indeed especially, on religious grounds. If I look at religion dispassionately, it must surely appear more and more as something that has human rather than divine origins. The people the church condemned were the very kinds of people that Jesus was attracted to, and who found love and acceptance from him. His ability and willingness to meet and accept people as they were is the very antithesis of religious bigotry. Such people could have found sad comfort in the fact that the people who condemned and marginalised them were the same people who crucified Jesus Christ.

Because religion tends to emphasise human endeavour, rather than divine initiative, there can be a great stress on quantity in worship, rather than quality. It can involve the spirituality of addition, rather than the spirituality of subtraction. By piling on more and more prayers, I can hope to climb the ladder of holiness! There is a failure here to realise, or to accept, that holiness is something that *happens* to me, rather than something I myself can generate or accumulate. Once again, in a very subtle form, we see original sin in operation where we assume to ourselves something that belongs to God. Religion, in the worst sense of that word, is trying to run things according to our rules and expecting God's approval for our efforts. Jesus came to replace the love of law with a law of love. He came to replace the ten 'Thou shalt nots' with two simple commands about loving God and neighbour. He came to show that God is a God of love, who is not into condemnation, rules, regulations, and retribution. He came, in other words, to do away with what is worst in religion. He came to replace religion with spirituality, and to tell us that God is more interested in what's in the heart than in anything we do. He came to free us from the bondage of legalism and perfectionism. We say 'Lord, by your cross and resurrection, you have set us free …'. How free we would be if we really believed that!

Summary for Reflection

Religion is what results from turning the divine initiative into human endeavour, and putting the emphasis on *what* we do and *how* we do it.

CHAPTER 5

Spirituality

Spirituality is about surrender, just as religion is about control. Spirituality is what God does, when we let him. In many ways, it differs fundamentally from religion. It is about something that happens in us, and through us. It has to do with love, not law, and it frees rather than binds. Spirituality is the result of Incarnation in my own spirit, where God himself is allowed to take over, and do for me what I could never do for myself. It is about becoming a channel of God's power, rather than a generator of that power. It is restoring the initiative to God, as I decide not to continue playing God. In simple words, it is about getting out of the way, and letting God do what he does best.

At the moment of creation, God breathed his spirit into the clay, and human life began. Later, that divine creation was damaged through original sin. Now God had a choice. He could scrap the whole plan and just forget about it. He could begin all over again, as if his first creation had not happened. Or he could take the damaged nature, and through his infinite love, create something beautiful from it. There is a legend about God as the master composer, and conductor of the orchestra of the universe. The wind instruments were entrusted to the wind. The percussion section was allocated to the seas, and to the thunder in the clouds. The trees, reeds, and grasses provided the string music, while the trumpets, whistles, and pan pipes were given to the birds and the animals. There was just one free agent in the whole orchestra, humans, and God decided that he would give them the freedom to blend with the harmony of the music, and trust them to use that freedom responsibly. In a way that would enhance the overall effect. God composed the most beautiful piece of music, and he proceeded to conduct all the elements in the playing of it. The effect was enchanting, the music was heavenly, in every sense of that word. Suddenly, one day, there was a harsh discordant note, that echoed throughout God's creation. Every instrument went totally silent with shock, and there followed a pause of spellbinding silence. 'What was that?' was the whispered question that went from one element to the next. Soon the whisper came back that it was the humans, the one free agent in the orchestra, and that had shattered the melody and harmony of God's composition. 'What will happen now?' whispered the trees. 'Will he tear up the score, and discard the whole exercise?' 'I think', says the wind, 'he will rewrite the whole score, and begin again.' 'One thing he cannot do', said the birds, 'He cannot go on, and pretend that nothing happened, because that discordant note is going to ring throughout his creation for all time.' And what did God do? He reached into the midst of all the sounds that had been, and took out that discordant note on its own, and, using that as a central theme, he wrote the most beautiful melody around it. The new masterpiece was based entirely on what had been destructive, and ugly, and it was now a thing of beauty, and a joy forever.

Spirituality is about re-creation, it is about God taking over and undoing the harm and damage resulting from our pride and arrogance. In the words of the hymn, 'Something beautiful, something good … all my confusion he understood. All I had to offer him was brokenness and strife, but he made something beautiful of my life.'

God took the damaged nature and breathed his Spirit once again into it, and human nature was restored to a greater beauty still. The only difference now is that each individual person has to say 'Yes' to that offer, if Incarnation is to take place on a personal level. The Spirit and power of God is *offered* to each individual, but it is up to each one to accept or reject that offer. Mary asked 'How can this be done?', and she was told that 'The Holy Spirit will come upon you, and the power of the Most High will over-shadow you.' Mary said 'Yes' to that, and, so, Incarnation took place in her.

Let's suppose my car was stolen. Let's suppose, further, that the car was recovered, and the person who stole it was brought into my pres-ence. What would I do? How would I react? I don't really know, but I do know how God would act. God would forgive the person, give him the car, and supply him with the petrol for the rest of his life! Crazy? Well, that's what God did. Original sin was us trying to become like God. God forgave the sin, and then devised a plan, through Incarnation, that enabled us come to share in his life, and he then offered us the Holy Spirit (the petrol!) that would enable us continue to live with his power. In all of this, God's love becomes so prodigally gener-ous that it is not possible for the human mind to comprehend it. Once again, part of the work of God's Spirit is to reveal that love to me. That is why it is true to say that saints are not the people who love God, but those who are con-vinced that God loves them.

I meet people who ask me how I am, and I don't really answer their question honestly, because I feel that they really don't want to know. Other people ask me the same question, and I answer them honestly. It is not the question that matters, but the spirit that inspires the question. Today, I might call you a clown, and you would know I'm being facetious and funny. Tomorrow, I could call you a clown, and you could be deeply hurt, because now you know that I really mean what I say. It is never the *words* that hurt or help, but the *spirit* in the words. If God's Spirit is in my own words and actions, then I can expect to be really helpful and healing. Like St Paul, I have to 'learn to live and to walk in the Spirit.' Living with the power of the Spirit gives me the force of inspiration and enthusiasm. 'Enthusiasm' comes from the Greek word 'Theos', meaning God, and it implies having God within, as I speak and act. Living a spiritual life means to live in constant awareness of God's Spirit and power within, giving me a force for good that I could never have by myself. I need only speak and act, and trust that God's Spirit in my words and actions will bring about whatever effect God wishes, in the circumstances. Mary didn't actually *do* anything. She gave God full permission to do whatever he wanted, through her. She is the perfect example for us in living a spiritual life. Mary did, in a perfect way, what the Lord would love to be allowed to effect in us.

It is very significant that, at the very moment that Jesus went down into the Jordan river, the Holy Spirit was seen to come upon him in visible form. At the moment he accepted all the brokenness, he was anointed with the power. Jesus came up out of that river, and again and again we are told how real and everyday the presence of the Spirit was with him. He was led by the Spirit into the desert, he was led by the Spirit into the temple. When the disciples returned to report on their first mission, we are told that Jesus was filled with the joy of the Spirit. He was constantly telling his disciples of the Father's love and care for them. Towards the end of his life, when he was getting ready to leave them, he spoke at some length, and with great earnestness, of what would happen when the Spirit came to them. He went so far as to say that they would do even more than he had done. The Spirit would teach them many things, as well as reminding them of all he had told them. The Spirit would accompany them, and comfort them. The Spirit would guide them along the way he had laid out for them, and they would never be alone in their struggles. The Spirit would give them the words to say, as they spoke to God and to others. They would be able to live by the power of God, and they would finally be led out of the power of deceit and darkness, into his kingdom of truth and light.

St Paul claimed that, before his dramatic conversion, he was the most zealous of his contemporaries in the ways of religion. He did all within his power to abide by each and every rule of his religion. And then, an extraordinary thing happened. God chose him, he said, to go to the Gentiles, and *show* them the good news about Jesus Christ. Being constantly aware of the *living power within* was Paul's way of describing what kept him going. He said that, when someone became a Christian, it meant to become a brand new person *within*, because a new life had begun. In other words, Incarnation had arrived in that person's heart. 'We are building a people of power' says the song. The power of the Spirit is to us what the spinach was to Popeye the sailor! There is nothing impossible to God, or to those who live by his power.

Spirituality is about being *gifted*. The many gifts of the Spirit are available to those who strive to live and to work in the Spirit. The gifts of the Spirit are freely available, to help me know, do, and say. This ranges from wisdom, to faith, to prophecy. I will always have access to the gifts. When my work is for the Lord, or of the Lord, I can be sure that the appropriate gift will be available in every situation. If I act as God's spokesperson, I can expect the gift of prophecy to anoint my words. If I counsel or make decisions, I can expect the gifts of wisdom, discernment, and knowledge. There is a gift for each occasion, and I am but a channel for those gifts, to reach out to, and to touch the hearts of others. These gifts, in turn, produce the fruits of the Spirit, which, in practice, is holiness. It is all the work of the Spirit, where God is directly involved in doing his work. Spirituality is, basically, about surrender, about turning my will and my life over to the care of God. Human nature is not to be trusted, because of its admixture of selfishness and self-will. It is only when I am guided by the Spirit of truth that I can have any hope of avoiding all the traps of self-deceit that are 'natural' to the human spirit.

Incarnation happened when the Holy Spirit came upon Mary, and Jesus was formed within her. At that moment, God's word of love began to take on flesh and to live among us. When Jesus was born, the cry went out that we would live for evermore, because of Christmas Day.

Oh happy fall that brought about such divine intervention. God visited his people to redeem them. Our sin and powerlessness were given eternal reprieve. Both the sin and the power-lessness would remain, but now there was a power at our disposal that would more than compensate for all of that. Where we were weak, now we are strong, because God's power is seen at its best in human weakness. What had been a problem is now an opportunity. Away, then, with original sin, in *all* its forms, especially when, disguised as religion, it would have us trying to save our own souls and merit our own salvation. Jesus came on earth to do exactly what the Father asked him. When he had completed that task, he then returned to the Father. He sent the Holy Spirit to complete his work. As the fourth Eucharistic Prayer in the Mass says, 'That we might live no longer for ourselves, but for him, he sent his Holy Spirit as his first gift to those who believe, to complete his work on earth, and to bring us the fullness of grace.' We now live in the era of the Spirit, and, in modern language, the Holy Spirit is now the executive branch of the Blessed Trinity! It is the Holy Spirit who gets things done around here any more. Spirituality is just an all-inclusive word that covers the situation, when we try to live by that simple principle.

Spirituality is about handing the initiative back to God, and avoiding all temptation to run the show myself. It is putting the stress on what God is effecting in me, and for me, rather than on anything I am doing for God. Even prayer becomes what God is doing, as I listen. It becomes far removed from 'saying prayers', and, even when I do speak, I am depending on God's Spirit, and the emphasis is much more on listening than speaking. Holiness becomes what happens to me, rather than anything I achieve through human endeavour. To switch the emphasis from religion to spirituality is one of the most freeing and liberating experiences the human heart can know. It becomes part of the experience of becoming one of the children of God.

Summary for Reflection

Spirituality is what God does in and through us when we hand over to him and let go of our own need to run things ourselves.

CHAPTER 6

Heaven

One of the focuses of religion is to get us into heaven. Usually, that implies going up to heaven, somewhere far above this earth. In childhood, we were told that heaven was a *state or place*. In practice, I think that the concept of a *place* is the one that holds the upper hand. This concept is further imbedded when we speak of Incarnation as God coming *down* among us here on earth.

Traditionally, religion has stressed rising above our humanity and brokenness, because there wasn't a whole lot of goodness and wholesomeness to be seen 'down here'! I think it rather amusing that, as soon as Jesus went out of sight of the apostles on Ascension Day, two men in white appeared to them, and asked them, 'Why are you looking up?' Jesus had stressed many times that he would henceforth be found in the broken, the marginalised, and the outcast. He also said that he was to be found all around us. Even a cup of water given his name took on an eternal value. Once again, it's not *what* we do, but *why* we do it, that is stressed. It is more about the *spirit* that inspires the action, than the action itself. Jesus gives a pre-view of what our final judgement will be all about. It will be about feeding the hungry, clothing the naked, and welcoming the stranger.

A lot of religion is seen to be very *vertical*, between God and me. Effectively, Jesus is saying that this is useless, unless it moves on to becoming *horizontal*, between me and others. The symbol of the cross in Christianity is highly significant. What comes from God to me, must go sideways to those around me. Unless forgiveness goes from me to others, it ceases to come from God. I must strive for a balance between the horizontal and the vertical. The more forgiveness, compassion, and understanding I extend to others, the more I am opened to a greater outpouring of all of that from God.

Sometimes, religion can be seen as building a stairway to heaven. In the Book of Genesis, we are told that the people built a very high tower that reached into the sky. They intended to live in it, and to be in control of their own destiny. God, however, thought otherwise, and he scattered them to the four winds. We are, essentially, a pilgrim people, always in the process of growth and evolution. Life is a constant dynamic, and can never become static. God, as creator, is always creating, and there is an on-going evolution as his plan and purpose continues to unfold. In bridging the gap between earth and heaven, God effected, through Incarnation, that heaven would come on earth. There are two parts to this rescue plan. The first is what Jesus did, and the second is that we accept what Jesus did for us. Paul says that our salvation lies 'in his blood, and our faith'. Jesus was saddened that the sin of this world was unbelief in him. He offers us salvation, and he surely hopes that our pride will not continue to insist that we earn or merit that through our own efforts. When we speak of Jesus, we often use past tense. 'By your cross and resurrection you *have* set us free ... Dying you *destroyed* our death, rising you *restored* our life ...' When Jesus did what he came to do, he returned to the Father, and he left the rest of the work to us.

Puccini was writing the score for the opera *Turandot*, when he felt that death was approaching. He commissioned his pupils to complete the work if he himself failed to complete it. He died before the work was finished, and his pupils took on the task entrusted to them. They studied his work in great detail, got a strong feeling for its spirit, and they finished the score. To this day, it is not possible to detect where the Maestro left off and his pupils took over. In a way, that gives an idea of our role as Christians. Jesus came to bring light to those in darkness, to feed the hungry and to bring hope to those in despair. In practice, my vocation has much more to do with me being available to the Lord to get heaven down here, than to be striving to get myself into heaven.

There are people on this earth who are living in hell. My vocation as a Christian is to bring heaven to them. 'Lord, make me a channel of your peace. Where there is hatred let me bring love ... where there is darkness let me bring your light ... where there is despair let me bring your hope ...' Not having time to bring heaven to them, because I am too concerned with getting to heaven myself, would be to get it very wrong indeed. As the hymn says, 'God has no other hands but yours ... no voice ... no feet on earth but yours ...'

Jesus gives us a preview of the general judgement, in which the questions will be scandalously materialistic. We will be asked about food when he was hungry, about clothes when he was naked, about a welcome when he was a stranger. There will be no questions about religious experience or ascetic endeavour, about hours in prayer or days in fasting. If those around me did not benefit from my prayers or my fasting, then such an investment of time may be seen to have produced little by way of eternal interest.

The old blacksmith was the only one of his trade in the whole valley. Everybody came to him with their broken farm implements. The people were very poor, and everything had to be repaired and kept in use as long as possible. One poor farmer died and left a wife and young family. At the same time, the Lord sent an angel to the blacksmith to tell him that God wanted him to come and live in his kingdom, that his sojourn on earth was over. The blacksmith sent the angel back to God with a heartfelt petition to be allowed to stay on for a little longer, because he needed to care for the widow and her children. Many years later the angel came again and, once again, the blacksmith was very involved in helping another poor family who had fallen on hard times. This was repeated several years later. Eventually the blacksmith got very old and feeble and this time he sent for the angel. 'Tell my Lord,' he said, 'that I am very tired and of little use to anyone around here, and that I would now like to go and live in his kingdom.' The angel smiled and replied, 'All these years past, when you helped the widow and protected the orphan, when you fed the hungry and gave to the poor, all those years you *were* living in God's kingdom. The only difference now is that the Lord wants you to share in the joys and rewards of the kingdom, after spending so much time sharing in the building of that kingdom.'

The kingdom of God is *now* and those who live by the rules of that kingdom are living in it now. In that kingdom, Jesus is Lord, everybody is important, even the most marginalised, and God's Spirit is the only power needed for living there. I believe that what we call the kingdom now will be called heaven later on.

There is nothing I'll get when I die which I am not offered now. Jesus said he would not leave us orphans, and then he went on to offer us his Father and his Mother. All that is needed from us is to become like children and to trust him to keep his promises. From an early age, children are taught to share and the importance of sharing. I knew of one little girl who refused to eat her dinner because she wanted her mother to send the food to all the poor starving chilren she had seen on the television. Her wish may not have been very practical but the spirit was right.

Jesus came to heal, and we can all be involved in the healing ministry. I can heal with a smile or with a hug. I can heal with five minutes of my time, or with a handshake. Just think of the many and varied ways in which people hurt each other. For every action or word that hurts, there is one that heals. I can be involved in building bridges that unite rather than walls which divide.

The biggest obstacle in my life to all of this is what is happening within my own heart. In life, the miles stretch out ahead, but the things that mess up my life are within me. The day I feel good about *me*, I think *you* are OK as well! God help you, though, on those days when I don't feel too good about myself! Unless heaven first enters my heart, there is no way I can be a channel of it for others. 'Let there be peace on earth and let it begin with me,' is a prayer that has come from reflection. What a sad contradiction to see a very religious person who is cantankerous and contrary and who deeply resents being taken away from, or distracted at, a time of prayer.

The old monk was praying in the chapel when the Lord appeared to him. He was in a rapture of pure delight when the doorbell rang. The monk knew it was a beggar because this was the time of day when they called in great numbers. He left the Lord and went to attend the beggar and, when he came back, he was amazed and delighted to see that the Lord was still there. The Lord explained that he would certainly have disappeared if the monk had chosen to stay with him rather than attend to the beggarman at the door.

Looking around the world today, it might be really difficult to see heaven there. I believe that such a vision is reserved for people of faith only. God's kingdom came on earth that first Christmas Day and, indeed, not many people saw anything different in that ... then, as well as now. Jesus came to give sight to the blind, and real blindness is that which prevents us seeing what really matters. It is very much the work of the Spirit to open our eyes to such a vision of the world. There is a raging battle today between the forces of good and evil, between the kingdom of God and the kingdom of Satan. There is a spiritual arms-race on for the souls and hearts of people. The Christian believes that, no matter how things may appear, evil can never triumph, even if it is seen to be successful for a while. The only real sin is to lose hope and to fall into despair. Jesus speaks of us being a leaven in the community, of being the salt of the earth and the light of the world. If the salt loses its savour everything goes bad. Salt is a preservative and, without it, rottenness can set in. We must let our light shine and not hide it under a bushel, otherwise the whole world is in darkness. One candle can effect the darkness in a very large room. 'Better light a candle than curse the darkness' is a solid Christian axiom.

I was in a position recently to be in close contact with a group of children preparing for First Communion. I liked everything about what they did but I was particularly impressed by the catchy songs they sang. First Communion was 'One more step along the road we go'. They sang about being happy, and showing it. In other words, if I'm saved I should begin to look saved! They sang a really catchy tune called 'Heaven is in my heart'. I envied them, getting such good news so early in life! I found myself hoping that the old traditional expressions and emphases of religion wouldn't catch up with them and rob them of the joy of what they had received.

There is nothing that I will receive when I die that I am not offered today. I can have God himself living in my heart, and I can live and walk in his Spirit. Jesus offers me his peace, his joy, and his abundant life. It is not a question of 'Live, horse, and you will get grass'. God really wants me to begin to share in his banquet right here and now. What a pity that I should let my stubbornness and pride get in the way, and live my life in a purgatory of my own making. It's my opinion that, when they die, most people go to purgatory. I believe they go there because they expect to go there. Why should God disappoint them? God will never disappoint me; he gives me the answers I expect. If I don't expect him to answer my prayer, then be assured that he won't. Scripture speaks of living 'with that sure and certain hope'. I really believe that to live this hope, and to give witness to this hope, is to be a very real light in the darkness of today's world. Such living must surely take on an eternal value. I believe that God does not send us anywhere when we die; I believe that he eternalises the direction we decide to take now.

Summary for Reflection

In practice, for us Christians, it can be much more difficult to get heaven into people than to get people into heaven.

CHAPTER 7

Hope

Hope is about God continuing to write straight on crooked lines. On a human level, the fall was a disaster, and all of God's great plans for his people were in ruins. His people ended up in exile in Egypt, as their plight continued to deteriorate. Life seemed to go from bad to worse for them. The extraordinary thing about them, though, is that they always retained a hope that all would be well. In their darkest moment, they spoke of a Messiah, who would come to rescue them from their misery and slavery. Throughout all their years of wandering through the desert, they never lost sight of that hope. They carried that hope with them when they were in exile in Babylon, and they longed for the day when they would be free at last. Their prophets continually reminded them that God would come to their rescue, and that all would be well.

All their hopes were fulfilled in Jesus Christ. The tragedy was that they failed to recognise the Messiah when he did come. 'He came onto his own, and his own received him not'. They had externalised their hope, and they thought of it as some sort of strong earthly power that would drive out their enemies and recapture their land. They failed to see that the freedom being offered was, first and above all, internal, a freedom from the inner slavery to self-will and despair. The Lord's work always begins in the human heart, before becoming evident in a people at large. The inner slavery, engendered by earthly ambition and greed, is a very subtle form of slavery, that is so much part of the human condition that it is not easily detected.

On that first Christmas morning, the heavens were filled with excitement and song, as a Saviour was announced who would free his people and redeem them. The prophet Isaiah had said that the Messiah would be recognised when the blind could see, the lame could walk, and the poor would have good news preached to them. Later, when John the Baptist's disciples came to Jesus to ask if he was indeed the Messiah, he replied, 'Look around, and see for yourselves. The blind can see, the lame can walk, and the poor have good news preached to them'. Yes, indeed, the Messiah had come and 'to those who believed in him he gave the right to become children of God. All they needed was to believe in him.' From that moment on,

Jesus went in search of those in darkness, those who had no hope, and those who were lost. The widow of Nain was alone in the world. Her husband had died, and now her only son was gone. It was a dark day, indeed, for her ... that is, until Jesus walked into her life. Everything changed utterly and for ever at that moment.

There was a dark cave deep in the earth that had never seen light. One day, the sun invited the cave to come up to visit it. It did so, and was so delighted to see light that, the following day, it invited the sun to come visit it, because the sun had never seen darkness. The next day the sun came down, came into the cave, and looked around. Then the sun asked, with puzzlement, 'Where is the darkness?' Once the sun had entered the cave, the darkness disappeared.

It was the same when Jesus came on earth. The little woman in the crowd had spent every penny she had over the previous eighteen years, and was no nearer to getting better. Another person had spent thirty-eight years at a pool-side, in the vain hope of being healed. Along came Jesus, and their lives were totally changed. As Jairus accompanied Jesus along the road towards his home, where his little daughter was seriously ill, there must have been some hope in his heart. However, when a messenger arrived with news that his daughter had died, poor Jairus must have got a real attack of panic. Jesus must have noticed that fact, because he whispered to Jairus, 'Don't worry, just trust me, and your daughter will be well'. Jesus' presence was like a steadying hand that was held out to Jairus at his moment of least hope. Situations like these best illustrate for us just what the presence of Jesus in this world must mean for the Christian. Zachary, the father of John the Baptist, said that Jesus was coming as 'a light to those who sit in darkness, and in the shadow of death, to guide their feet into the way of peace.'

On a human level, Calvary was a very dark day, indeed. As Mary stood at the foot of the cross, she needed all the faith and hope she had, to believe that this was not the end. As with the journey to Egypt, at an earlier time, she believed that this was part of some greater overall plan of God, and she knew that all would be well, in God's own time. This kind of faith comes from leaving all the major decisions in life to God, and trusting that he knows what he is about, and that he always has everything under control. Without this re-assuring conviction, we would be completely lost, and would continue to stumble along from one crisis to another. Easter morning was the confirming of her faith, and I like to think that she was not at all surprised on that occasion.

When Jesus caught up with the two disciples on their way to Emmaus, they were very despondent indeed. Jesus brought them back through the Scriptures, where all of this had been foretold, and he chided them for their lack of faith. He must surely have been disappointed that they should have lost hope, in spite of all they had seen him do and heard him say. It was very important that they should continue to have faith in him, and not lose heart. He had made very clear and definite promises to them, and it was vital that they believe those promises. Elizabeth told Mary that 'all of this happened to you, because you believed that the promises of the Lord would be fulfilled.' Once again, in the words of St Paul, it is what Jesus has done for us, and our belief in the reality and consequences of what he has done.

In a way, one could say that what happened on Easter morning was confined to Jesus only, and no one else was immediately effected by it. Pentecost Sunday was *our* Easter Sunday. On Easter day, the stone was rolled away from the tomb, and Jesus came forth, having successfully passed through death, into a life in which death was non-existent. On Pentecost morning, the doors of the Upper Room were thrown open, and the apostles went forth, imbued with a whole new life, ready to take on any struggle on this earth, confident that, at the end of the day, all would be well. They were no longer the craven cowards who had barricaded themselves in a room for fear of the Jews. They now had a new courage and a new hope, and they knew that they now had, within themselves, a power much greater than any evil powers they might meet on the road of life. They began to experience and to share in some of the victory that Jesus had gained. Jesus had overcome the three enemies of sin, sickness, and death. Jesus had told them that, like a branch growing out of a vine, they could draw on the life that was his, and they could live with the power that he had. They knew they now had a power so much greater than themselves, and that would enable them live a life beyond their wildest dreams.

Peter and Judas had fairly similar experiences. Both gave Jesus the thumbs-down, as Judas chose the money, and Peter opted for his own security. The similarity, however, ended there, as each tried to deal with what had happened. Judas committed the ultimate sin in thinking that he had put himself outside of the Lord's forgiveness. He lost hope and went out and hanged himself. It is significant that, as the gospel tells us, 'when Judas took the morsel, Satan entered into him ... and he went out and hanged himself.' Earlier, Jesus said he had come that we might have life and have it to the full. Destruction and death, without hope, is surely the hall-mark of Satan. In this, I do not pass judgement on someone committing suicide because I believe that, in most cases, this must surely be the result of a brain-storm, or of life going into a tail-spin and getting out of control. Peter, on the other hand, retained his hope in the Lord's forgiveness and love, and he repented of what he had done. Later, in his letters, he gives a very positive directive to the early Christian church, 'Always have an explanation ready to give to those who ask you the reason for the hope that you have.'

In other words, as Christians, you should always have hope, and you should always be able to give others a reason for that hope. I really believe that a very positive hope, even at times of uncertainty and doubt, is an important part of Christian witness.

Christianity and guilt are incompatible. Guilt is not from God, and can be very negative, and pessimistic. In the Book of Revelations, Satan is called 'the accuser of the brethren; he accuses them day and night, before God.' It serves Satan's purpose that we should be burdened with guilt, and that such guilt might accumulate, to become such a heavy burden, that we might lose hope, and despair. I believe that *despair is the only real sin a Christian can commit.* My reason for saying this is that despair might prevent me bringing something to the Lord and letting him take care of it, just as he readily deals with anything else we bring to him. To believe that anything I have done is outside of his love and forgiveness, is to fly in the face of everything Jesus has told us, and, like Judas, to compound the situation by letting go of the hope that must always accompany us. That hope must always be held in sight, no matter how much we fail. I believe that such hope must surely out-weigh all, and any, of our human weaknesses, failures, and sins.

There is a vast difference between being helpless, and being hopeless. The difference is so great, that I might say experiencing and accepting helplessness can be a virtue, while admitting to hopelessness can be a sin! The whole Christian message is about God coming to us, in our helplessness, and making it possible for us to live by his power, with a whole new hope, and offering us a life beyond our wildest dreams. The paradox of this is that, the more conscious I am of my own powerlessness, the more powerfully the Lord can work in me. Like St John the Baptist, the more I can decrease, the more the Lord can increase. The more I can get out of the way, the greater free-dom the Lord has to work in me, and through me. I could easily fall into the trap of trying to have faith in *my* faith! I could easily over-emphasise my own contribution to all of this and, thus, get in the way of the Lord. My hope is based on Jesus, and on him only. It is based on his love and on his promises, and not on anything I can do, or have done.

Life can be difficult, and there are times when it's not easy to retain hope and optimism. I am only human, and it's quite normal to have my good days, and my bad days. The hope I speak of, however, is part of the work of the Holy Spirit in my soul and is total gift that tran-scends all my human weakness, and is *in* me, rather than *of* me. It is one of the fruits of the Spirit, or the results of the Spirit living in me. If I see a tree with apples on it, I will rightly con-clude that it is an apple tree. If I see the fruits of the Spirit in your life, I will rightly conclude that you have the Spirit within you. 'You will receive power from on high', Jesus promised his apostles, 'and you will be my witnesses to the ends of the earth.' In other words, you will receive the power, but you must also accept the responsibility that goes with such power. Showing, in all situations, the hope that you have, is very positive Christian witness. It's a long journey from the fall until now, and throughout that time, there is constant proof of the Lord's care and concern for his people. Even within the relatively short span of my own life, I must be able to recognise many signs of his care and concern for me. To think of what time may be left, and to leave that to him, is not a great deal to ask for. I can continue to worry, of course, but, as Jesus said, 'Will all this worry add one minute to your life?' In fact, with the rise of heart attacks, heart failures, and other coronary problems, it is accepted that worrying and good health do not go together at all! Worry could well be defined as resulting from a lack of faith in God. 'All will be well and all manner of things will be well', is a saying attributed to St Julian of Norwich. What a wonderful Christian motto that would make! It deserves to be repeated here, as a very fitting conclusion to this chapter. *All will be well, and all manner of things will be well.*

Summary for Reflection

I can never be outside the embrace of God's love and forgiveness, and the greatest thanks I can give him for caring for me up until now, is to trust him to see me safely to the end of the journey.

CHAPTER 8

Church

In our history books, the letters BC and AD, distinguishing the eras before and after Jesus came among us, do nothing to convey the tremendous nature of that change-over. Since the coming of Jesus, nothing has been the same. God, in Jesus, had taken on a body like ours. We could touch each other, hug, walk, and weep together. The body Jesus had was very central to everything he did. He needed a body for the ordinary everyday human contacts he made. He touched the leper, hugged the children, and broke the bread to feed the hungry. He used his hand and his voice, as he asserted his authority over the storms and the demons. He walked the length and breadth of the countryside, and he wept with those who mourned. He was a visible, tangible presence of God among his people. People fell at his feet, and touched his garments. After the resurrection, he ate food, and asked Thomas to touch his wounds, as evidence that his body was still real, and that he was living in it. When he ascended to his Father, he brought his body with him.

In a sense, his real work would now begin. Now he needed another body, a way of being tangibly present in another way. His followers were asked to supply that body, and, of course, he would supply the Spirit, or the power for that body to continue his work on earth. That new body is what we call the church. The early church was called 'the company of believers ... the followers of the way.' Through them, he would continue his work and bring it to completion. In his name, they also would feed the hungry, heal the sick, and give sight to the blind. Jesus had come 'to do and to teach.' Firstly, he did, and then he taught his disciples what to do. He washed the feet of his disciples, and he instructed them to do this for each other. He wouldn't ask them to do anything he himself had not done.

Let's pretend, for a moment, there is no church. I read the gospels, and I ponder them. Then I wonder if this would work, so I set up an experiment. I select a group of people at random who are willing to join me in this experiment. The first condition is that each one in the group would be different from the others. We are going to form a body, and if they were all the same, we would end up with a whole lot of heads, or hands, and no other parts! The second condition would be that each person accept the fact that all the others are different. When other people annoy me, it is usually because they keep doing things I wouldn't do! However, we must now accept the fact that God made all the others different from me, and that's just the way it is. The next thing to stress is that each person is uniquely gifted, and, in forming a body, those gifts must be made available to the rest of us. God gives me nothing for myself. He doesn't give me my gift of speech to go around talking to myself! Community is like a mirror that is taken from a wall, let fall, and shatters in many pieces. Each person in the group is given a piece of the mirror. Each one reflects God in a very different way. The idea of community is to encourage each one to contribute the piece of the mirror entrusted to him or her, so that, as we put the mirror back together again, we may reflect the face of God. Our witness value is what matters. We must be seen to be united. 'By this will all people know that you are my disciples, if you love one another.' At the Last Supper, Jesus prayed, 'Father, I pray that they may be one, as you and I are one ... so that the world may believe that you have sent me.' The whole witness of who Jesus is, and where he came from, is dependent on the evidence of our unity.

The Spirit is not given to the individual. It is

given to the body, and it is only to the extent that I am a committed member of the body that I am open to the full outpouring of the Spirit. Before Pentecost, the apostles gathered with Mary, the mother of Jesus, in an Upper Room, and they prayed 'with one mind, and one heart.' It is in this that the Spirit becomes operative. The purpose of the Spirit is to form the body, to blend the members in unity of purpose. 'See how these Christians love one another', was the observation of the on-lookers, as the early church unfolded. Without this witness, the church has no purpose, and becomes an obscenity that must surely appear like idolatry in the eyes of God. If I come across the body of Christ without the wounds, I know it is a phoney. There will always be wounded people among the Christian community – the alcoholics, the drug addicts, the socially maladjusted. How the church deals with such is vital in its witness as the body of Christ. There can be no such thing as a 'sanitised' church, where everything is cosmetic and correct, and where unpleasant realities are handled with forceps! The church is Jesus present, here and now, where, once again, he touches the leper and befriends the prostitute. Unfortunately, over the years and the centuries, the church may well have been seen as more on the side of law than of love. There is an historical explanation for this, but, of course, it must not excuse it. The church is, first and foremost, for sinners; a place where the sinners will find love, forgiveness, and welcome. Ideally, coming to the church, to the Christian community, should have a sense of home-coming about it, where the hymn rings out, 'welcome all sinners ... come home.' As a Christian church, we need to make a clear distinction between condemning injustice and wrong-doing, and having real compassion for the sinner. We must love the sinner, while condemning the sin. If you have a son or daughter not going to church, you, as a parent, will not have to account to God for that. All you will be asked is 'Did you still love your children, whether they went to church or not?' That, I believe, is the acid test of the church's authenticity: does it still hold out a hand of friendship, and present a friendly face whether people avail of its services or abide by its rules? Jesus said that he had not come to condemn anyone. Neither is it the mandate of the church to issue anathemas, or to ostracise people. I am saddened when I reflect on the high self-righteous moral ground that the church was seen to follow over the years.

My vocation, as a member of the Christian community, is the same as Mary's. I am asked to make myself available to form the body of Christ. To my every query, I get the same answer as Mary, 'The Holy Spirit will come upon you, and the power of the Most High will over-shadow you ...' The big problem with this is that I cannot select and choose the other parts! It is really a path towards wholeness, or holiness. The Lord surrounds me with the very people who will make me holy. One person will make me very patient, the other person will make me very forgiving! There is no one in my life that I can do without, if I am to become complete, or holy. It is as if the Lord took the engine of a car apart, and spread out all the parts on the ground. To each one he gave a particular part, and the problem arises when I realise that, with what I myself have, and that alone, the engine cannot work! I need what the others have, if I am ever to become complete. Right from the start, God knew that 'it is not good that man should be alone.' It is almost as if God set out a programme that would leave no place for the do-it-yourself-by-yourself individual, who would live life independently of others, with reference to God, and him alone. Even, to this day, if someone feels called to the life of a hermit, such a one must be 'sponsored' by some Christian community, and approval and blessing must be received from the group, before the call is considered genuine. The hermit is never alone, because a genuine hermit goes aside to have time for God and for others. Such a person is the heart of the body, and the full-time prayer-life is for the glory of God, and for the building up of his body, the church.

I remember seeing the notice outside a church once, which had church spelt 'ch—ch'. Underneath was the question 'What is missing?', followed by the answer 'UR'! I also remember a congregation being asked to spell the word church out loud, with special emphasis on the two centre letters, 'c.h.U.R.c.h'. A church is made up of people, not bricks and plaster. A minister shocked his congregation one Sunday morning, by announcing that the church was dead, and the funeral would be held the following Sunday morning. The people turned up in great numbers, mostly out of curiosity. There was a coffin in the sanctuary, with the lid removed. The minister invited everybody to come forward to 'view the remains.' Imagine the surprise, when each one looked into the coffin, and saw themselves reflected in the mirror that lined the base of the coffin! They quickly got the message. For far too long, the church was seen to be made up of hierarchy and clergy. It was easy enough for the ordinary folks to criticise the church, because it was seen as something other than themselves. That fallacy still persists today and it may be some time yet before it is completely removed. There was a reason for this, because, to a large extent, the hierarchy and clergy acted and spoke as if they were the church. Nowadays, however, with the fall-off in vocations to priesthood, the laity have some hope of regaining their rightful place. The greatest need in the church today is the formation of the laity, when people are trained to accept and play a central role in the life of the community. This has begun, in some small measure, by the return of ministries, but, even that is but the tip of the ice-berg. Please God, the time will come when the clergy will be prepared to resume, and will be permitted to resume, their proper place in the church. This will be one of service, more than of authority. It will require a great deal of letting go, but with less and less priests around, we can hope that it will happen. It is not necessarily a good thing to have too many priests!

Change is part of living, and anything that is not constantly in some process of evolution and change, may well be dead. I believe it is part of the work of God's Spirit to constantly 'make all things new.' With half the world dying of hunger, I think it is obscene to make a central issue out of whether we should have girl Mass servers, or whether we should have guitars in church! We are supposed to be more about mission than about maintenance. I believe if we are about maintenance, we will die, and the sooner the better! If we are about mission, we will never die, because, it is right there that the promise of the Lord, given to his church, comes into play. It is when Jesus sent his disciples out on a mission that he made the most explicit promises about being with them, and guaranteeing that the gates of hell would not prevail against them. A lot of the pessimism that one hears from time to time about church, vocations, and where-we-go-now is very far from the hope that should be part of a resurrected people. The church is a pilgrim people, and we must continually be on the move, not wishing to maintain the status quo, but continually letting go of where we've been. Detachment is a Christian virtue, and when it includes everything but the Lord himself, it is most generous. Religious life, as I knew it, growing up, is finished, and we are now experimenting with new ways of living it. As one convent and seminary after another, puts up the 'For Sale' signs, we must be reminded of the many ruins of monasteries that dot our landscape, all from a previous age. One hundred years from now, there will be something else that will have come, and may well have served its purpose also, and is about to go. It is not for me to be concerned about such things, because that is all the work of God, and I must be reassured that he knows what he's doing. Ministry and service in the church is a charism, and God, who imbued the church at its foundation with all the necessary charisms, will never withdraw them. How they are expressed, and who is called to express any one of them at a particular time in history, is a decision that God has retained for himself.

These charisms, or gifts, are vital to the life of the church. The church is fully equipped by God, with every gift that is needed, divided among his people. The role of the community is to call forth those gifts, and to provide scope for people in the exercise of their gifts. As St Paul says not all are teachers, not all are prophets, not all are preachers. To each is given the appropriate gift, that, through exercise of those gifts, the body will be built up. Like the story of the talents, I will have to give an account of the gifts entrusted to me. There is a particular difficulty with this today, because the church has just begun recognising the responsibility of each individual within the community. The individuals, on the other hand, have little or no training in the exercise of their gifts. For far too long their role was to pay up, pray up, and shut up! However, we must be optimistic about this whole question. I honestly feel that we are on the way, and God always has time on his side. I may not notice any great fundamental changes in my lifetime, but I certainly have lived long enough to be convinced that a process of change is underway, and the future looks exciting. It is difficult for us to be patient with the pace of change, when the needs are so urgent, and many of the obstacles so evident. However, I believe in this is our merit, that we long and pray for change, that we speak our truth in love, and that we retain a vibrant hope in the midst of it all. Above all, I believe that it is important that I continue to develop a deep love for the church, and contribute to its up-building, through my work, and through my prayers.

Summary for Reflection

The church is the visible body of Christ on earth, and through membership of that body, we, as a people, give daily witness to the words and the works of Christ among us.

CHAPTER 9

Baptism

I was born into a family that was not of my choosing. I inherited genes, a name, parents, and siblings that I had not chosen. As I grew up, I was, inevitably, compared to a parent, a brother, or some other relative, with whom I shared a resemblance. For me, all of that was fixed, definite, and predictable. If I had been adopted at birth, much of that would have changed, without, of course, me still having much choice. My adoptive parents would have taken care of me, while waiting, with some anxiety, for my natural mother to sign the necessary papers, to finalise the adoption. In this case, the procedure would have been more deliberate, as some serious decisions were being made about my future. Finally, I now have a family, and the process of rearing me in security can begin. Those adoption papers assume a vital element in that security, and, no doubt, are preserved with great care. I remember being in a house one evening, where a few children had been adopted. At one stage, one little lad was rummaging in a drawer, in search of something. To his mother's question, he replied that he was looking for his 'papers'. When his mother asked him why he wanted them, he replied that one of his pals did not believe that he had been adopted, and he wanted to show him the proof. His mother pointed to another drawer, where the papers were, and armed with the proof, he rejoined his pal at the front door. It all seemed so natural, and healthy, and it gave me much food for thought.

In my case, I was brought to the church to be adopted into the family of God, through the sacrament of baptism. At the end of that ceremony, my parents were given a certificate of baptism, as proof to all the world that I had been adopted into the family of God. Later on in life, when I began school, I had to furnish this certificate, and again when I came to make my first communion and confirmation. It is one of the first things that is asked for when someone comes to arrange a wedding. The details of my baptism are entered in a parish baptism register, and preserved with great care. This register is much more than an historical reference book. It is official recognition by the Christian community that his person is, in fact, a member.

Returning to the idea of adoption, for a moment, it is remarkable how adopted siblings develop a family resemblance for the family of adoption. I have often remarked on how an adopted child assumes the traits, characteristics, and much of the personality of an adopted parent. 'Wouldn't you know them out of each other. Isn't she very like her mother?' are comments frequently heard. I refer to this for the purpose of reflecting on the family resemblance that is *expected* to show, after several years of adoption into the family of God. Jesus said 'I will not leave you orphans', and then he proceeded to offer us his father, and his mother. He went on to say, however, that it wouldn't work unless we became like children. Once again, I must stress that Jesus doesn't *give* me anything while *offering* me everything. The onus is on me to assume full membership in the family of God. In the case of adoption, the baby and the adoptive parents are powerless, and cannot have a future together until the birth-mother signs the official papers. This is a very serious decision, but for both parties named, it is not under their control. In the case of my baptism, however, it does not become fully effective until, at some future date, I personally, decide that, yes, this is what I really want. I cannot go on living on a promise made for me by someone else. The time must come when I take ownership of that decision. Through many ways, and especially through other sacraments, I will be reminded of those baptismal promises, in the hope that, as time goes on, I 'will become mature in my understanding as strong Christians ought to be', to quote the letter to the Hebrews. At key and significant moments throughout the church year, I will be invited to renew those promises, always in the hope that my understanding of them, and my commitment to them, will continue to deepen with time. I am always in process, never actually arriving anywhere, short of death. Chesterton said that we never really become Christian, we are always in the process of *becoming*. I believe this concept is very important. I remember, some years ago, attending some talks on mid-life spirituality, and the lecturer began with the following sentence: 'Most of you people here are fifty-something, and as we look again at the whole concept of Christianity, you may discover that now, at last, you may be ready to begin.' I felt like cheering, because he said exactly what I had in my heart!

One of the paradoxes of Christianity is that it is about living, and it is also about dying. Jesus said that he came that we should have life, and have it to the full. It is also about dying, in so far as, as a Christian, I can actually do my dying during my lifetime. The cross symbolises putting someone else before myself. The cross was intended for Barabbas, who represented us, but Jesus took his place, and Barabbas walked away scot free. Every time I put someone else before myself, I die a little to my own selfishness. Death is like a pile of sand at the end of my life, that I can take and sprinkle a little every single day, through the many little dyings that are part of Christian living. If I do that, I may well find that there'll be very little dying to do when I reach the end, because I may well have all of my dying over me. On the other hand, however, if I wait 'til the end of my life to die, it may well be too late. Water represented both life and death for the Hebrews. Water was their life-saver as they wandered through the desert for forty years. They had to pass through water to get into the Promised Land, just as well we all have to pass through death to get into the full-ness of life. We symbolise this fact through the use of water of baptism. We pour water on the person begin baptised as a symbol of the dying that lies up ahead, as well as the new life that re-sults from water being applied to things that grow. My own practice, in the baptism ceremony, is to catch the water in a dish, as it is being poured. At the end of the ceremony, I then pour the water into a little bottle, and give this to the parents. I explain to them that, for the natural completion and maturing of the sacrament, this water should be brought back to church, one drop at a time, every time I celebrate eucharist. At the offertory, I hold up the chalice of wine, that represents the chalice of suffering that Jesus accepted for us. Before I do that, I put a drop of water into the wine, to represent all my own human pains and struggles as I die daily, for the sake of those around me. By themselves, my daily dyings have very limited value, but by putting them in the chalice, and uniting them to the death of Jesus, they take on a redemptive and an eternal value. This is one of the many direct links between eucharist and my baptism.

Jesus said that he had come as a light to the world. He came as a light to those who sat in darkness, and in the shadow of death. Later, he would tell his disciples that they were to be a light to the world. He encouraged them not to hide that light, but to let it shine so that others might see their good works and thus give glory to his Father in heaven. When we celebrate the triumph of Jesus at Easter, we lay great stress on the centrality of light. We light an Easter fire, and we invite everyone present to light a candle from the flame of the fire, and hold that up for all to see. We also light an Easter candle, which remains in sight within the church for the remainder of the church year. When we prepare the materials for a baptism ceremony, one of the first things we do is light that Easter candle, and place it very close to the baptismal font. A candle will be lit from it and handed to the parents of the baby being baptised. This represents the light of Christ which is being entrusted to them to pass on to their child. At this stage, I may refer to the limitations imposed on us, through our constant experience of infant baptism. Much of the real significance and meaning is lost because the person being baptised is the passive one in all that occurs. This situation is being redeemed somewhat these days, through a ceremony of light that usually precedes confirmation. On this occasion, the parents are asked to hand on a lit candle to that former baby, who is now twelve years old, as a sign that they are passing on the light of the Christian faith. In most cases, the parents use the candle from baptism as a sign of the continuity of the process.

Oils are used in the baptism ceremony as a sign of sacredness and anointing. Oils have always been used as a symbol of anointing and commissioning. Kings were anointed on assuming the authority of their state. They are used at confirmation to signify the out-pouring and anointing of God's Spirit. The newly ordained priest is anointed with oil as he is sent forth to minister to God's people. And, finally, when a person comes close to moving into the fullness of life, in death, oils are once again used as that person is commissioned for the journey home to God. The journey that began in baptism is now complete.

In my own parish ministry, I always ensured that the coffin was placed on the baptismal font for all of the funeral ceremonies. Such witness helps reinforce the belief that baptism is central to the Christian journey. Baptism is, in fact, the basis of all my sacramental life. In practice, it is more important than my ordination. Ordination determines my role within the Christian community, whereas baptism brought me into the community in the first place. I love to highlight the baptismal font at a service of reconciliation. I have the Easter candle lit nearby, and those wishing to seek forgiveness and to begin again, are invited to come forward. After the prayers of absolution, a candle, carried by each person, is then lit from the Easter candle, and given to them, with the words, 'Receive again the light of Christ, and do your best with it this time!' Continuing the theme of the oil, I then anoint each on the forehead with oil. On Ash Wednesday, each is marked with ashes as a reminder that we are sinners. The use of the oil at this ceremony says that we are accepted and anointed by God, who, like the father of the prodigal son, is prepared to pour out the oil of gladness upon us.

There is a story told about the chief of a tribe somewhere in Africa. One after another, his family came forth for baptism. As each baptism took place, the missioner tried to get the chief to join the others, but to no avail. As it happened, all of his family came for baptism, but the chief continued to hold out. Eventually, four years later, the chief came to the missioner and requested that he be baptised. The missioner asked him, out of curiosity, why he wanted baptism now, and why he had held out when the rest of his family had come forward for baptism. The chief's answer was very simple, 'I waited to see if baptism would make any difference in the lives of the others. If it hadn't, then I didn't see any point in being baptised myself. Now I can see that it has made a great difference in the lives of my family members. That is why I am asking to be baptised.'

Yes, baptism is supposed to make all the difference in the world. The problem with sacraments, however, is that they are not automatic. Pouring water on someone doesn't make that person a Christian, no more than a couple saying a formula of any description in front of a priest is a guarantee that they will ever love each other. A sacrament is a decision, but it is more than that. John and Mary could decide to live together. That is a decision. They could, however, come to church, and sacramentalise that decision. *Now* they receive the grace from God to carry out that decision. That is a totally different story altogether. A sacrament is a decision, and it includes the grace or the power to carry out that decision. A sacrament is something that happens now, but it depends on the *future* to give it meaning. In other words, a sacrament begins *after* I go out the door of the church. I go through a certain ritual in the presence of the Christian community, and then, after I leave the church, I strive to give meaning to the promises just made. In the case of baptism, that involves the rest of my life. A sacrament can die. John and Mary, who eventually got married in church, could be still living in the same home, but their sacrament could be dead years ago. I could carry my baptism certificate around in my pocket all my life, but the sacrament itself may have been still-born. It is a mistake to confer any magic powers on sacraments, as if they work of themselves, independently of the person on whom the sacrament was conferred. It is a life-long struggle for the Christian to give life to this sacrament, and to keep it alive. All of the other sacraments, by their nature, continue to confirm the basis of our baptism. It is never a question of spiritual perfection, as much as spiritual progress. I said earlier that I will never *become* a Christian; I am always in the process of *becoming*. Membership in the Christian community, to which my baptism gives me entry, is something that continues to grow and develop over a lifetime. That journey will include many failures, and many occasions when I will wonder if I'm in the right shop at all! There is only one sin to commit at this stage – to give up or to lose hope. Salvation is the grace I get to start again. Our glory consists, not in never failing, but in getting up every time we fall. Baptism sets our feet on a path that is paved with eternal hope. It is important to hold on to this hope, when we are caught in the struggles and tensions along the way. These struggles and tensions are part of the journey for the Christian. If you waken up some morning, and your life is the way you had always wished it to be, don't move, just call the undertaker, because you have just died!

Summary for Reflection

As with adoption in ordinary life, adoption into God's family, through baptism, gives full privileges, access, and responsibilities within the family of adoption.

CHAPTER 10

Today

Life is a journey, and it is a mistake to judge the merit of the journey by its length, rather than its depth. There is a great difference between living and existing. Everybody dies, but not everybody lives. Some people skim the surface of life so superficially that, when they die, there is real need for a doctor to sign a death certificate as proof of death, because there was never much life there in the first place! Life is a mystery to be lived, rather than a problem to be solved. As with any mystery, there is a constant unfolding and on-going revelation. It is not possible to have an over-view of life, short of having the time and the lucidity on my death-bed. Time is always *passing* by, and as soon as I grasp hold of one moment, it is gone and replaced by another. It is not possible to slow down the process, or to make time stand still. Listen to the conversation of an older generation, and, usually, it has to do with 'the good old days', with a time that is past. The problem with this is, of course, that the time in question no longer exists, and the present moment is slipping by to join that by-gone time, and there's not a whole lot happening *now*!

Many people spend much of life on a cross, or in a tension, of their own making. One hand is stretched out into the past, trying to change it, while the other hand is out into the future, trying to arrange it. The problem here, once again, is that there's not much happening now. The only benefits of the past are the lessons it taught me. I would be very wise, indeed, if I learned every lesson life taught me. Unfortunately, many of us continue to stumble on into the same mistakes, and our experience of the past is completely wasted. I can learn from the past, and I can benefit greatly even from its greatest blunders and failures. Any compassion I have has come out of my own brokenness, and, with hindsight, I can see that any worthwhile growth in my life took place at times of struggle and difficulty. It is one of the attributes of God, that he never wastes a thing. He can turn our greatest sins into an eternal blessing.

In the *Serenity Prayer* we pray for the grace to accept the things we cannot change. I cannot change the past. Yesterday went away at midnight, and will never return. All the regrets, hindsights, and misgivings in the world will not change one second of the past. Jesus alone can make something out of my past, warts and all. When he bowed his head in death on Calvary, the effect of that reached back to the moment of creation, and forward to the end of time. He alone is the alpha and the omega, the beginning and the end. If I accept him as my saviour, he can take care of all my past, and I can leave it with him, without regret or worry. I sometimes think of the past as a room, full of everything that has been part of my history up 'til now. The contents of this room include many things from before my time – influence, biases, and bigotries that I inherited and that influenced me deeply. In my family tree, I cannot expect to inherit the good looks and the intelligence only. I inherit the whole lot, the good, the bad, the ugly. I need to open that door and invite Jesus to take over there, with a whip of cords if necessary. I ask him to redeem, to rid this temple, to exorcise this room, and to sprinkle it with his precious blood, for the forgiveness of every sin in it. I place the whole lot under his control and authority, and I drop the hand I had stretched out, trying to change it. I get out of that room, myself, as I leave Jesus in charge, no longer allowing myself to be a prisoner in the past. Jesus asks the question, 'And you, who do you say that I am?' I am saying he is my saviour, as I leave my past to his mercy. When I do that, I believe he takes all my sins and dumps them in the deepest lake. The problem for some people, who are pre-occupied with their sins, is that Jesus puts a sign on the lake which says 'No Fishing'!

Let us now look at the other arm that is stretched out, trying to arrange tomorrow. Once again, in praying for the serenity to accept what we cannot change, we must include every moment of the future. Jesus himself asks 'Will all your worry add one minute to your life?' The answer is that, not only will it not add to my life, but it will most certainly shorten it. 'Who'll push my wheelchair when I'm ninety?', is a worry from which I can get great mileage. It could be a great waste of time, of course, because I may not live to be ninety, and, anyhow, with the health cut-backs, there may not be any wheelchairs by that time. In the room of my past, I accepted Jesus as Saviour and left it all to him, and with him. In the room of my future, I ask Jesus to be Lord, to take over, and to run the show for me. I can go into the room of my past, and I can clearly remember much of what is there. In the room of the future, however, it is complete darkness because I cannot see up ahead. Jesus knows what's up ahead, every moment of every day of it. It is not predestination, because I do have a very clear choice. I can choose to go it alone, or let him lead me, and there is a world of difference between one decision and the other. I can decide to get out of that room, with all my worries about the future, and put Jesus in charge. When I do that, something extraordinary happens. Jesus breaks my life down into twenty-four hour segments, and, each morning, he gives me one of those out of that room. This morning, when I woke up, I accepted, with gratitude, a very special gift. It was the gift of *today*, never before given to a human being on this earth. There are many people, alive yesterday, who did not receive the gift of today. It is total gift, and written all over the box are the words 'batteries included'! With the day comes whatever it takes to live that day. Jesus called this 'our daily bread', and he told us to ask for that, and that is all we need for each day.

I can spend my life worrying about things that probably will never happen. I can be stuck in the past, or in the future, and there's not much of me here now. God, however, is totally a God of *now*. 'I am who am' God called himself, giving himself the quality of a continuous presence. Unless I become a person of *now*, I cannot meet God. Some people meet God for the first time in death, when the running has to stop and they come into an eternal now. George Burns, the American comedian, who celebrated his ninety-seventh birthday recently, says that he wakens up each morning, and the first thing he does is check the death notices in the paper. If his name is not there, he gets up! Each morning, when I am assured of today, I accept, with gratitude, the gift that it is, and get on with living that gift. At the end of the day, I then return it to the Lord, with renewed gratitude. As I pass it to him, in that room of my past, I trust him to take care of any failures that have been part of that day, and I leave it with him. Life, lived one day at a time, loses much of the stress that can wear out the system. It also can bring me into a daily awareness of the Lord's loving care for me.

There is a tendency to flex my muscles, grit my teeth, and clench my fists, as I make yet more promises to the Lord. The idea of living one day at a time helps me to come into a personal daily experience of the Lord's promises to me. Jesus makes very definite promises, and all he asks is that I believe those, and trust him to deliver on them. I have his promise that nothing will happen today that he and I, together, will not be able to handle. The gates of hell will not prevail against me, and I am assured that my name is registered as a citizen of heaven. He gives me full authority over all the power of the evil one, and he assures me that nothing will harm me. He promises not to abandon me, or leave me in the storm. It is much more a question of his promises to me, than any promises I might make to him.

Life is a process, and it is one of revelation and continual learning. I draw a line along the wall beside me, that stretches out beyond the horizon, and on that line I mark the more significant years of the normal life. At the beginning, I mark where the baby is born, and is learning to breast-feed or feed from a bottle. Later, the baby is learning to walk, learning its first sounds, and learning to hold things. The attempts at walking are often cut short, when a little head hits off the leg of a chair, and all sorts of loving is needed to reassure the little one that it is not the end of the world. The attempts at speaking are so pathetic that only the love of the mother can translate the sounds. And the spoon always seems to end up on the floor, despite attempts to hold on to it. All of this is part of the process of learning, and we do not, or should not attribute failure to the beginner's attempts. We readily admit that the feeble steps, the falling, and the crawling are all part of what is necessary, if the child is ever to be able to run around. If we follow the growth of the child, we will encounter the same process at work when she comes to learn to read, write, ride a bicycle, or swim. The learning process will involve getting it wrong as often as getting it right, and the great thing about this is that getting it wrong is just as central a part in the learning process as getting it right. What a pity that we do not extend that 'learning space' to the many other things we need to learn, to be able to live life with responsibility. If I move along the line to the spot where I myself am at now, I must ask myself 'What am I learning right now?' I must be just as much in the process of learning as when I was a baby, or a small child. I may be learning to listen, to be honest, or indeed, to live one day at a time. I have to *learn* to keep my life within the day. To learn means practising, and it involves day-in day-out repetition. Like the child learning to walk, I will get it wrong many times, but I have got to stop thinking of such times as failures. If all the process, the ups and the downs, bring me, eventually, to living today, with none of me back in yesterday, or off into tomorrow, then there has been nothing but resounding success. If I am not learning, I am not living. This learning process must continue to the day I die. The central lesson to be learned in living within the day, is that my confidence in God's care for me, and my faith in his promises to me, must grow with each day. Faith is a response to love. The more I am convinced that someone loves me, the more I come to trust that person. Faith must also make its way down into my feet, because, in my head, it is often little more than mental assent. To believe that Jesus is God is not virtue, because even Satan believes that. That belief becomes faith when it gets down into my feet, and I begin to step out to do things, and to say things, because of that belief. If you have a car to be serviced, and I recommend a friend of mine. I tell you that he does an excellent job, his price is very reasonable, and he is totally reliable. If you decide to leave your car with him, you are doing so because you believe what I told you. You are acting on *belief*. When you get your car back, you discover that he did an excellent job, and his price was, indeed, very reasonable. The next time your car needs a service, you go back to the same mechanic, but this time you are acting on *faith*, because now you know that all will be well. It is the same with learning to live one day at a time. In a very short time, I will have crossed the bridge between belief and faith, and, in doing so, I will have begun to enter into salvation.

There was a programme on an American television station one time that took place in a su-permarket. Four women with shopping trolleys were lined up and, at the sound of a whistle, they were to dash around the aisles in the sup-ermarket, filling the trolleys with produce from the shelves. At the sound of a second whistle they were to come to the check-out area, where the value of the goods was established, and the person with the most valuable trolley was de-clared the winner. The scene in the check-out area was chaotic, as each checked what the other had got. There was a general feeling of disappointment, as different people were heard to say, 'Oh, why didn't I pick that? Why didn't I take more of those?' and so on. So much like the ways of the world! Now let us make one change in the line-up, as we give a fifth trolley to a committed Christian. The whistle sounds, and the scramble begins. This time, there is a different scenario. The first four dash from shelf to shelf, grabbing goods by the arm-full, while our friend proceeds slowly from shelf to shelf, taking a loaf of bread from one, and a pound of butter from another. She picks up items dropped by the others, and places them on their trolleys. Eventually, all five return to the check-out area. Four of them have trolleys laden down, and piled up with groceries, and are completely out of breath, while the fifth is laid back and relaxed, with a trolley that has two or three items. This really annoys the others, and one of them turns on her, with a look of scorn, and disbelief, as she asks 'What are you doing here? Surely you know this is a competition? Where are you going with those few items?' Our friend smiles, and replies, 'Actually, my father owns the supermarket'!

When I learn to trust my Father to provide what I need, as I live each day, there is no need to get involved in the rat-race. I now have joined in the children of God, and I begin to experience the freedom that comes with that.

Summary for Reflection

Today is life in miniature, from the time I am born, through awakening in the morning, to the time I die, as I fall asleep at the end of the day.

CHAPTER 11

Wholeness

I have chosen the word *wholeness* over several other words that springs to mind, meaning the same thing. I could use the words *wholesomeness, holiness,* or *togetherness,* but *wholeness* seems to better say what I have in mind. I am mindful of using the word *brokenness* quite often in the earlier part of this book. Wholeness includes brokenness, rather than excluding it. Wholeness is what happens to the brokenness when it is made available to the Spirit of God. Wholeness is about reconciliation, about balance, about coming together. The work of the Spirit is, essentially, about reconciliation, acceptance, and forgiveness. It is about calling together all the parts, and healing the alienation that comes from guilt, and religious intolerance.

I am a unit made up of several dimensions, physical, spiritual, and emotional. It is a mistake to stress any of these to the exclusion of the others. A worry in the mind becomes an ulcer in the body. There is a direct connection between all the parts. God created all of me, and he knows that all of me is good. My earlier up-bringing and formation may have laid a wrong and, indeed, unhealthy stress on one of these to the detriment of the others. In my own case, I understood that my head could be hanging off, but that was all right as long as my soul benefited from the suffering! I was told that feelings, while actually not sinful, were dangerous and must be kept under wraps at all time. The body was certainly a mine-field, that must be whipped into submission and docility at all costs. Christianity was about giving without counting the cost, working without seeking rest, and fighting without healing the wounds. When I reflect on that now, I am indeed grateful to be as sane as I am!

The approach to which I refer came from an understanding of a very strict and demanding God. That approach was very much part of religion at that time. It was tied in with *us* running the show, and achieving our own salvation. God was demanding, and we were performing. God was recording each thing we did, said, and thought, and we would have to render a full account of all of that when we met him face to face. This would, of course, generate a great amount of guilt, and it was almost impossible to *feel* forgiven. Because I myself was playing the God-role in my own salvation, I could always be depended on to pile on the guilt until I lived in almost constant fear, and in an unhealthy relationship with God, myself, and, consequently, with many others. Wholeness is about calling home all of those areas of alienation, and allowing my heart to become the meeting place for sin and salvation, for wretchedness and redemption, for the human and the divine.

My personality is made up of the sum total of all my habits, good and bad. I inherit a great deal of this, more of it is absorbed in my early childhood and adolescent environment, and, of course, through the behaviour patterns I develop in life, I add my own personal contribution. Most of it comes from nature and from nurture. I am not at all saying that I should not take responsibility for my behaviour. What I am saying is that the better I understand my behaviour, and why I act as I do, the better I am able to deal with it. It is not about guilt trips, or about laying blame. It is about understanding, accepting, and taking healthy responsibility. The Enneagram is a method used to look at personality types, and why we do what we do. It tells us that there are nine types, and I belong to one of those, with perhaps a part of me in one of the others. These types range from the perfectionist to the indolent, from the aggressive to the helper. It is generally accepted that, in early childhood, I adapt to the type that will guarantee me the highest hope of survival in my environment. If being good is appreciated, I will develop the helping *persona*. If perfection is what is expected, I will strive to meet those expectations. If aggression is the name of the game, I will learn to fight my corner as good as the best of them. Each personality type has its good points and its weaknesses. For example, number two in the Enneagram is the helper. However, this ranges from the healthy two, down through the average two, to the unhealthy two. If you sneeze, the unhealthy two will run for a tissue, but will also want to blow your nose for you, and, if you do not permit this, is deeply offended that you do not appreciate all that is being done for you. In other words, such a person is meeting a personal need to be helpful, and thus running your show, rather than really helping you. What I'm saying here is that it is good to know where I stand in all of this, so I can begin to deal with it in a healthy and constructive way.

The proper approach to God is to open out the canvas of my life ... fully ... fully ... right out to the edges. Don't hide anything, because God sees it all anyhow. However, he can do nothing with what he sees until I open it out to him, and invite him to get involved. He stands outside the door, with hat in hand, and will not enter until I open the door. Fear of rejection, in the past, might have hindered this approach. Indeed, God may have been expected to stand back until I was finished, and then give his approval to what I had accomplished. God looks over the canvas of my life and he sees it all, the good, the bad, and the ugly. There is no condemnation in God, because we are part of what he created in love. Through Incarnation God has shown himself to be at home with brokenness. In fact, he can make his home in the midst of it all. I am convinced that his great wish is that I would learn to feel more and more at home with myself. Wholeness is about being at home with myself. Freud said that a test of a person's maturity is his ability to be alone with himself for any length of time. Many people find it difficult to be in their own company for any length of time. Go into most kitchens any morning, and don't be surprised that the radio or television is providing a background noise to whatever work may be going on. The same is true of the factory floor, or the canteen. There may not be anybody actually listening to the radio or watching the television. It is just that the extra voices serve to distract me from the awkward silence that is part of being alone with myself. It is reckoned that solitary confinement, long enough, is the only sure way of driving a person insane.

What's going on inside my head, my heart? Where is the anger coming from, and where are the resentments directed? It is very necessary to get in touch with what's going on. So often, anger gets misdirected and comes out in all the wrong ways. It's like a man coming home from the office, and kicking the dog inside the front door. The anger is towards his boss, but the dog serves as a release valve. Sometimes, indeed, the anger is towards myself, and the person who hates himself shows this, usually, by not having a good word to say about anybody. Despite all the people around whom I can blame for things that are wrong in my life, most of what messes me up in my life is inside me.

A man pulled into a filling station, and asked the attendant what the people were like in the next village down the road. The attendant, who was nobody's fool, asked him how he found the people in the last village he had come through. The man replied that they were very friendly and helpful. 'Well', said the attendant, 'you'll probably find that the people in the next village will be the same.' After a while, another motorist stopped by and asked about the people in the next village. When the attendant asked about the people in the last village, he was told that they were sour, dour, and unfriendly, to which the attendant replied 'You'll probably find the people in the next village to be just that way, too.'

Prayer is at the centre of this journey towards wholeness, or holiness. The work is actually the work of God, but, in prayer, I place myself at God's disposal, to receive direction and guidance from him. Prayer should not be just functional, where I am striving to obtain or to achieve something. Prayer can be an end in itself, where there is nothing more happening than just wasting time with God. It can also involve reflection, because a life without reflection is not worth living. It is not about achieving or accomplishing anything, because, in real prayer, God is the actor. In the summer I may go out into the back garden on a sunny day, dressed or undressed accordingly, and just sit in a chair to get a sun-tan. All I am doing, actually, is showing up, and letting the sun come to me, in the knowledge that the sun will effect the results I seek. The more and more 'at ease' with God I become, the less reason I have to perform or to conform. Hopefully, as the

Spirit rises up from within, bringing more and more issues to the surface, the acceptance I experience in prayer will be shared by me towards myself, and I will begin to share in a divine and healing gentleness. The Spirit is always at work in the depth of my being. A woman who is pregnant can best understand this idea. As each day goes by, she is more and more conscious of a life stirring within. She is most conscious of this when she is alone, and is more in touch with what is happening. This is a very good analogy for prayer, when I can go aside, be still, go downstairs into the core of my being, and get in touch with what is happening there. My more helpful response to this is my whispered 'Yes', repeated again and again. Wholeness is what happens to me, and within me, when I allow it.

In a symbolic way, my hands should be open in prayer, as a token of an open heart. The more gentle and unforced my approach is, the more reconciliation is taking place in me. If I go out after a shower of rain, I will notice areas that are already quite dry, and other areas that have pools of water. One place is quite loose and relaxed, and the water soaks in, with little difficulty. The other areas are tightly packed, and intense, and the water cannot penetrate. It is something similar with ourselves. 'Be still, and know that I am God' is a phrase of divine wisdom. Jesus sought any opportunity that came his way to go aside to be by himself, or to take his disciples aside to rest awhile. As with God, so with good friends, I can waste time very constructively and profitably. When I free myself from the delusion that I am here on this earth to live up to the expectations of others, I have taken a direct role in my own redemption from the slavery that comes from people-pleasing, and approbation-seeking. People like myself, that are involved in ministry to others, have been trained to give and to be available to others, without reference to our own needs. To give any priority to our own needs was construed as selfishness and neglect of duty. I remember hearing a story one time about Carl Jung, the famous Swiss psychologist. A lady of wealth and prestige came to him one day to make an appointment for the following day. Jung said that he was not available the next day, because he had a very important appointment that he just could not break. Despite her attempts to coax, persuade, and bully him, he held out, and insisted that he was not available. She left him, highly incensed. The following day, she was being driven along the shore of a lake, when she spotted Jung walking along by himself close to a cluster of trees. The next morning she was waiting in his clinic when he arrived, and she proceeded to berate him for telling her lies about the important appointment he said he had for the previous day. Jung, quite unpreturbed, told her that he always had an appointment with himself every Wednesday afternoon, and that was one appointment that he would not miss for love or money.

Wholeness is about gathering all of the brokenness, in love, and spreading it all out in front of me. It is allowing the warmth of God's love melt the hardness, heal the hurts, and reconcile the alienation. It is about coming together in the warmth of his love and acceptance, and of beginning to share some of that love and acceptance with him.

I heard a story from a missioner home on holidays from Africa. Once a month, he used to go out into the bush to round up all those in need of surgery, and bring them to a clinic he had, where the flying doctors arrived at regular intervals. Those in need of similar type surgery were collected each time. On one occasion he rounded up all those with hare lips and cleft palates. The doctor would arrive, and do many such operations in the same day. One young lad, with a hair lip, had a very successful operation and the improvement was dramatic.

When the time came for him to leave the clinic, the missioner brought him out to his father, who was sitting beneath a tree waiting for him. The boy stood in front of the father, and bowed to him, as the father placed a hand of blessing on his head. What amazed the missioner was that the father seemed to pay no attention to the obvious transformation that resulted from the surgery. Then the boy went towards where some women were waiting, and their excitement knew no bounds. They brought him into a hut, and produced every available light to closely examine the results of the doctor's handiwork. They were clearly very excited as they clapped, and hugged the boy with delight. The apparent apathy of the father was highlighted even more by the joy and excitement of the women. Eventually, the missioner approached the father and asked him if he were not pleased with the wonderful job the doctor had done on his son. The father said he was very pleased with the results of the surgery. The missioner then asked him why he had not shown any of that pleasure when he saw his son for the first time after the operation. The father's reply was simple and to the point. 'I love my son', he said, 'and if I showed any sign that I was greatly excited about what has just happened, it would show that I love him even more now that he has no hare lip. This would surely mean that I had not really loved him just the way he had been up 'til now.'

If that man could apply the very same approach to himself, as he struggles along the journey of life, he would, indeed, have reached a wonderful level of wholeness.

Summary for Reflection

God would really abandon the ninety-nine strengths and virtues in me, to go after the one part in me that is alienated because I will not 'own' it and allow it to come home, where it belongs.

CHAPTER 12

Death

I often joke that death is the greatest kick of all, that's why it's kept 'til last! Life on this earth is a journey from one birth to another birth. Just as the cord is cut at birth, so are the straps pulled up out of the grave at the funeral. I move from the womb life, to the womb of life, to the fullness of life. That third, or final, stage of life is what I was created to be, and when I pass through death, I will then be what God had in mind all the time. When I was in my mother's womb, there was no way that I could understand her. I had to wait to be born, to stand back from her, to really look at her. It was accepted that I actually looked like her. I am now in the womb of God, this time being formed in the image of Christ. I cannot understand God. I am like a tiny fish in the Atlantic ocean, swimming around, encountering new experiences of the same sea every day. It would be a foolish little fish, and a very dead little fish, if it tried to rise up above the sea, and get an overall view, from coast to coast.

The body is not me. I am living in the body for a relatively short while, and, when the proper time comes, I will leave the body and go on to the next stage. What is left is called 'the remains', and it matters little whether that is buried, cremated, or left for donor organs. I will never go into a coffin. The body is like the booster rocket on a space shuttle which, once the shuttle is launched and given direction, can then be discarded and fall back to earth. If I drew a line along the ground, and off to the horizon, and then put two marks on the line, a few inches apart, that would represent the fact that I spend but a tiny part of my existence in the body. Life, once begun, never ends, but goes on into eternity. At the moment of death, when I leave the body, I will be free for the first time in my existence; free from all of the restrictions and limitations of the body. One definition of a good life is that, when I was born, I alone cried while everybody else was very happy. I should live my life in such a way, that, when I die, I will be happy, and everyone else will be crying. Or, as Mark Twain said, 'Live your life in such a way that, when you die, even the undertaker will be sorry!'

There is a vast gap between the three stages of life. If the unborn baby could hear you, there is not one word you could use that the baby could understand, with its limited intelligence and experience. Similarly, if someone came back from the third stage, there is nothing of that state that I could understand. 'Eye has not seen, nor ear heard, what things God has in store for those who love him.'

In the bottom of a lily pond, a small group of grubs were discussing life now and life hereafter. They remarked that, as each grub climbed to the top of one of the lilies, none ever returned to tell what it was like. They agreed among themselves, that the next one called to the top would come back to tell what happened. Soon afterwards, one grub felt drawn to the surface and he began climbing the stem of a lily, with a firm promise to return and tell the others what it was like. When he reached the surface, he crawled out on the green leaf of the lily and looked around. It was so bright up here; it had been so dark below. It was also pleasantly warm. Suddenly, something began to happen to him as he opened out and was transformed into a beautiful dragon-fly. He flew back and forth, across the pond. He could see the others below, but they couldn't see him. He tried to return to them, but found that this was not possible. After a while, he gave up trying, remarking to himself that, even if they could see him, the change had been so extraordinary, that they would never recognise such a beautiful creature as ever being one of them.

Death is central to the life of the Christian. We say to Jesus 'Dying you destroyed our death, rising you restored our life.' Death was the final enemy for Jesus and, by passing through death, and returning to show this at great length to his disciples, he was quite insistent that death was no longer an enemy for the Christian. St Paul's problem was that he longed to die, but he felt obliged to remain on for the sake of the people in his care. He resolves his problem by concluding that, as he belonged to Jesus, it mattered little whether he lived or died. There is nothing I will get when I die, that I am not offered today. Jesus offers me his Father, his Spirit, his mother, his peace, and his abundant life. Water represented death for the Hebrews, as they passed through the Red Sea to enter the promised land. Jesus walked on water, to show that he had full authority over death. Peter asked if he might have that freedom, and Jesus beckoned him to step out of that boat. Unfortunately, for Peter, he became more preoccupied with the waves than with Jesus, so he panicked and began to sink. For the Christian, there is no other way through life, or through death, than Jesus, who said that he was *the Way,* and no one could come to the Father, except through him. The early Christian church members were called 'followers of the Way'.

St Thérèse of Lisieux and Padre Pio both said that their real work would begin after they went on to the third and final stage of life. I believe that, mostly from my own experience. On several occasions, I gave responsibility for some family or individual to a dying person, telling them that he/she would soon be in a position to do much more than I could hope to do down here. I was never once disappointed as I watched for the improvement I myself had long struggled to achieve. Could anyone say that Jesus or Mary ceased to bother about us once they entered into that final stage of the journey? It makes all the sense in the world that the good should continue to be effected except, now of course, with much greater effect. In a literal sense, a Christian is an eternal optimist and, while living this present part of the journey, is fully conscious that the best is yet to come.

Funerals have more to do with the bereaved than with the person who has died. The readings, songs, and homily at the Mass are directed towards those present. There is a healing that can take place, for those bereaved, as we slowly and with deliberation, go through the ceremonies of final commendation and committal. Ask someone who has lost a loved one, where a body was never found, and who has not had the benefit of going through this ritual, and you will discover just how healing a funeral can be. Grief is the price we pay for love, and if you don't want to ever cry at a funeral, then don't love anybody, because that is the price you must pay. If you have any capacity for love, then ensure that you have plenty of tissues handy! Jesus wept at the grave of Lazarus, but they were tears of love, not despair. Bereavement is a process, a journey. There is no short-cut through the process. It is like losing a leg by amputation. I will walk again, but it would be wrong to try to do so too quickly. Just as each person is unique, so is the bereavement for each person. I can never really say to another 'I know what you are going through.' Usually I don't, and am just putting on the other person an experience that has been uniquely my own. Being present with the bereaved, and being a good, sympathetic listener, is often the best help I can give at such times.

In Irish, we have a hymn which says that the seed, the harvest, and the haggards and barns, into which the harvest is gathered, all belong to Christ. Life is often about saying 'Yes' to

God, at various stages along the way. The greatest 'Yes' of all is that final one, if I have an opportunity to say it while still of sound mind. Quite often, we are not sure what to do with death. We are unsure whether we should approach it realistically, or wait 'til it approaches us. One thing is sure, we will all die one day. It is much safer to keep that in the first person plural! I will die one day, can be too close for comfort!

Jesus took on the three evils of sin, sickness, and death. It is literally true to say that he could not possibly have done more for us than he has. It is in our growing relationship with him that we learn to entrust him, more and more, with those things that trouble us. He is our Moses, bringing us through the desert of life into the Promised Land. He has guaranteed never to abandon us, but to be with us, even to the end of time. It is sad to hear Jesus say that the sin of this world is unbelief in him. When the Son of Man comes, will he find any faith on this earth? In other words, do I believe what Jesus tells me? Salvation is about what Jesus has done for me, and whether I trust him to deliver on those promises.

I remember, many years ago, speaking to an old lady and asking her about death. I asked if she ever thought of death, and she said she thought of death every day. I asked if she was afraid of death, and she said that she certainly was not. Then I asked what death meant to her, and she said it meant meeting all her old friends and never having to say good-bye again. Never having to say goodbye again ... I reflected, at a later moment, just how much of life is taken up with partings and saying good-bye. Death must be the most freeing experience a human being can have. With Martin Luther King we could shout, 'Free at last, free at last. I thank my God, we are free at last.'

Summary for Reflection

When I pass into that third and final stage of life, I become, for the first time, everything God created me to be, and intended me to be.